STUDENT'S GUIDE TO SUCCESS

Cartoons by George Middleton

Student's Guide to Success

W. Fisher Cassie, C.B.E.,
Emeritus Professor of Civil Engineering,
University of Newcastle upon Tyne

T. Constantine
Professor of Civil Engineering,
University of Salford

M

© W. Fisher Cassie and T. Constantine 1977

First edition 1977
Reprinted 1978, 1979

Published by

THE MACMILLAN PRESS LTD

London and Basingstoke
Associated companies in Delhi Dublin
Hong Kong Johannesburg Lagos Melbourne
New York Singapore and Tokyo

Printed in Great Britain by
Unwin Brothers Limited
The Gresham Press, Old Woking, Surrey

British Library Cataloguing in Publication Data

Cassie, William Fisher
   Student's guide to success.
   1. College students — Conduct of life 2. Success
   1. Title II. Constantine, T
   378.1'98   LB3605
   ISBN 0-333-23277-1

Contents

Preface

The techniques of note-taking, study, examination, oral exposition and other important means of communication are usually developed casually and ineffectively in students of tertiary education. This book is a distillation of many seminars held, during the last couple of decades, in the Universities of Newcastle upon Tyne and Salford. Throughout we have used the term 'College' to mean university, polytechnic, teachers' training college, sixth-form college, adult education college or any other institute of higher education.

The chapters are as 'light-hearted' as the importance of the topic permits, to encourage students to try at least some of the ideas presented. We are grateful to friends who have helped us: to George Middleton, for his amusing sketches, to Joan Shaw, for typing all the manuscripts, to Zita E. Henderson, for her help with mnemonics in chapter 2, to Ethel Parkinson and Audrey Lumb, for their advice on chapter 5, and to Basil Rogers, for his splendid description of the 'on-going situation' in chapter 6.

W. Fisher Cassie

T. Constantine

Acknowledgements

The tables on pp. 49–51 are reprinted from Edition 18 Dewey Decimal Classification and Relative Index (1971) by permission of Forest Press Division, Lake Placid Education Foundation, owner of copyright.

1
Coming Clean

Well, I suppose you could say I really *was* a successful student — first class academic results, running for the College, first bassoon in the Orchestra (what a joke!), and all that. But this didn't happen because I was brilliant. Once you've met a really brilliant mind you realise people like us are small fry. But we can still be successful.

In the end I really enjoyed College life. Not many can say that for every facet of College society — study, sport, social activities, and so on. It all happened by repeated dragooning — not by me: I couldn't have cared less that first term, I was so miserable. Nothing went right and I nearly gave up. You see, I'd been accustomed to the guided progression of the last comfortable years at school. Of course, there were exams which had to be passed to let me into College but these were accomplished by hard, but guided work. I was kept on the rails.

With the first weeks of College my illusions were shattered. This was no super-sixth-form with teachers guiding me smoothly on to the higher reaches of learning. Games did not appear in the curriculum. Lecturers did not appear to bother whether I attended their lectures or not. There were great gaps of time when no one directed me at all. I asked one lecturer 'What do you wish me to do now?' and his answer was 'That's for you to decide. What did you come here to do?'

Scrappy notes of lectures piled up unread and kept pouring in

Thank goodness we had tutors who helped us to some extent and who seemed quite accustomed to listening to tales of woe. But so much pressed in; so many matters demanded attention at the same time! A meeting of the Committee of the Rambling Club, an essay or a report to prepare for next day, some knotty maths problems that seemed to have no solution, a party in the Junior Common Room, notes from a lecture on particle physics which needed tidying up (Dr Glib talked so fast!). It went on and on until I was nearly frantic, so I went out for the evening several times in one week to release the tension.

Well, you can imagine what happened! I took the easy way out. Scrappy notes of lectures piled up unread and kept pouring in. I bought the prescribed or recommended books but had no time to read them. I enjoyed training sessions on the track or circuit training in the gym. I dropped in on long sessions of talk, putting the world to rights — after all that was supposed to be one of the main aspects of college education wasn't it? I got fed up working in the library on fine autumn days and went cross-country running. And then eight or nine weeks after my happy entry into College I was on the carpet — kindly chat, of course, but none the less serious for not being a court martial! Home I went for the Christmas vac with the ragged tatters of what should have been a well-moulded start to a brilliant career! Some career, I said!

Well, there you are, I've come clean. That's what happened. How did I recover from the débâcle? After all, if I can get a book published as a 'successful' student there must have been a dramatic change in my outlook. You might like to hear what happened. No, it was nothing to do with being taught the great learning of the world. I was simply given some down to earth instruction on *techniques*. That's a bit of a come down isn't it? Nothing special about that you might say. But read on.

Work Study

It happens that my father is one of the top people in what is known as *Work Study*. This type of study is what it describes — the study of how to work. It is aimed at getting the most out of available time as is possible without distress to the person working — at least that seems to be the rough definition. My brother, sister and I used to scorn Pa's 'stop-watch slavery' as we called it and drew sketches of him whipping his work people to faster and faster production until they dropped with exhaustion. We were all for 'Workers of the world unite'!

When I got home for Christmas he just said 'What about listening to me now? Unless you learn how to control your work and recreation you'll come an almighty cropper and it will be your own fault.' Mind you, he didn't force me, but I knew that even successful businessmen asked his advice, so perhaps I might find out what this study of how to work was all about. So I asked for help; I didn't like doing it but it seemed necessary. He was pleased and relieved.

My second term after Christmas was much smoother as a result but it still held problems. However, a more careful analysis of methods of work and recreation in the Easter vac helped me to overcome these problems and be more in charge of myself, rather than being tossed about at random. It all developed from *techniques* — routine methods of doing the basic fundamentals so that they became automatic. Of course, for the deep thinking necessary in advanced topics my 'brilliant' ability came into play! It all took time but worked out in the end.

Success Depends on Effective Communication

This phrase was the first point made by father. It burned itself into my brain from his eternal reiteration. He pointed out that whether I was listening to a lecture, writing an exam, taking in the instructions of a track coach, studying in silence, reading a book, writing an essay or a report, or laying down the law in a pub, communication was operative. I had to develop communication methods which became so automatic, so intuitive, that facts, ideas and opinions flowed easily and effectively without loss of time between me and the rest of humanity living or dead. No, nothing spiritualistic! — dead authors still communicate as you read. *The ability to communicate effectively in speech and in writing is one of the most important attributes I had to cultivate* — said father. 'Success' he remarked 'is not a matter of chance — how many hours are there in a week?' I didn't know at once. 'O.K.' he said 'you haven't even thought about your basic asset — time. You don't know the first thing, do you?' Pretty devastating, I thought, and nearly walked out.

Effective Communication Depends on Technique

This word 'technique' was father's favourite. I got really fed up hearing it and thought that one more repetition would send me screaming down the street!

Technique is knowing exactly what to do and how to do it *fast*.
Technique is being so practised in the application of a method that
there is a smooth and *fast* action, and results are immediate.
Techniques are routine and detailed methods of carrying out specific
tasks *fast*.

He went on like that; really he did! The word 'fast' kept cropping up. 'You
don't want to waste your life do you?' he said. 'How many hours in a week?' I
knew this time; I was progressing.

Techniques, he said, need repeated practice. The racing motorist, the
concert pianist, the wood-carver, the learner preparing for a driving test — all
need to learn techniques and to accomplish them *fast*. Why should a student
be the odd one out? Studying, writing an exam, playing for the University,
speaking in a debate, writing notes, achieving spare time for leisure — all
need techniques so that time is not wasted.

Basic Techniques

As father said at the beginning of gruelling sessions in the vacs, the techniques
I needed for the next few years — apart from those concerned with sport —
dealt not so much with manual skills but with communication, both written
and oral.

He said there were three groups into which communication techniques fell

O I L

Output, Input and Links

Output

If you don't know what you want to communicate you can't make anyone else
understand. Seems obvious when it's put that way. One professor was heard
to remark 'I really don't know enough about that subject. I shall give a course
of lectures on it.' To be sure that he understood, he was willing to prepare an
adequate output.

Input

The output prepared must be meaningful to the hearer. The input, which is
the same material from the recipient's viewpoint, must be adapted to his

ability to absorb it. A lecture on nuclear physics prepared for the Royal Society would not be a suitable input for a Rotary Club Lunch.

Links

Communication of related ideas must flow on lines of proved techniques; there must be adequate links between the constituent parts.

Father got a bit worked up about this, but it was above my head until I got down to the specific steps to success which appear in the following chapters, so just remember OIL. Like me, you'll begin to see what it means when you get a bit further on.

Personal and Impersonal Communication

Father said 'We'll restrict ourselves to *speech* and *writing*. These are your two tools. Develop their techniques; use every means to cut down the time used up. Practise techniques.' All right, O.K., he had been going on long enough on these lines. What next?

It was in the first Easter vac that he produced *The Table*. Look at figure 1 at the end of this chapter and cover up the last column. You'll then have some ideas of what I was up against. He showed me the Personal/Impersonal and the Individual/Group columns all drawn out as in figure 1 but the last column was missing. 'Now' he said 'write down all the detailed types of communication you think can take place while you're in College until the end of your courses and put them in the right parts of the chart. Well, I ask you — what a nerve!

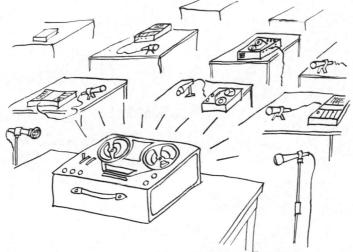

The ultimate in impersonal communication

If you haven't cheated and have really covered the last column, you'll be lucky if you manage to get ten examples down and in the right places. I managed eight. When I did see the full list I was very scornful — speaking in public? making a recording? conducting a committee? — ME? But they all eventually happened and I'm even writing a textbook. I got one back on father all the same. He left *Personal speech from a group* blank. He said I wouldn't be up against an angry mob at my age. Poor father — not 'with it' is he? He'd no idea of what happens in a demo!

How to Use the Book

From now on I'm not going to chat to you any more. The subject is too important. I'm going to adopt the editorial 'we' and you may then pay more attention than you would to the burblings of a recent graduate.

Of course, I didn't follow every one of father's edicts — who could? But I noted them all down with the dignified 'we', for he and I now agreed. In the end, I really did have a good time at College. *Work, sport and social activities* ran easily side by side, There was time for them all — after I'd absorbed father's time-mentality. In the end I had to admit he was right and I'm still extending and using the ideas where they apply to my present job.

Be sure to do the bits at the ends of the chapters.

Good hunting!

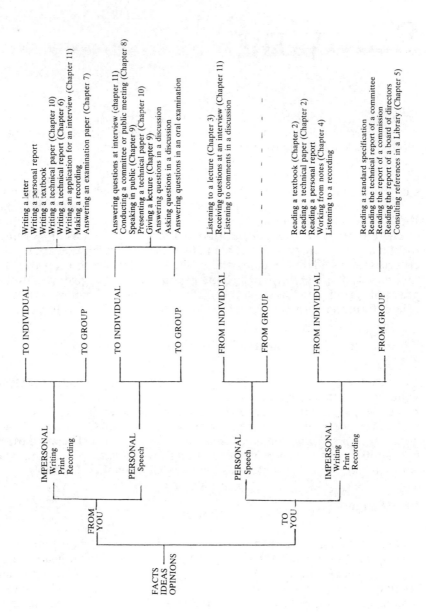

Figure 1 Ways we communicate

2
Studying

Of all the steps in communication, studying is probably the most irregular, uncontrolled and impersonal, and yet is of immense importance. Your study should result in the active absorption into your mind of accumulated and recorded knowledge. It is only on this body of knowledge that you are able to build your further development. To you the task is daunting; the act of studying is hardly one of compulsive fascination. Reluctance to embark on it is commonplace. Personal contact is missing during study hours, and the chore is a lonely one. Yet this step in communication is the key to all the rest.

There is no paucity of advice. Books discuss the theories of learning, the psychology of teaching and study, and the practical methods of applying these criteria to the student's circumstances. We have decided to keep away from a theoretical treatment in this chapter and simply to give you well-tried practical techniques that have been found to work. Findings, firmly established, form the basis of discussion. Neglect our advice at your peril.

The Techniques of Study

Your study will be effective only if you are prepared to apply intelligently to your work certain well-known techniques, most of which have been used successfully from time immemorial. To help you keep in mind the five main techniques we have invented a mnemonic, MACRO, which stands for *Memory, Aims, Concentration, Review* and *Organisation.* The word MACRO is easy to remember since it means *being exceptionally prominent,* which is surely the aim of every ambitious young person reading this book.

M: Memory

Memory training is much discussed these days, and several popular books have been published on the subject, some with extravagant claims built into the titles. However a word of warning: good as these books are for giving you techniques to help you remember strings of unrelated facts, numbers or words, they do not in any way show you how to train your memory to remember other facts in a different context. A simple true story will illustrate this point. Some years ago we lent to a colleague a memory-training book with a very attractive title, which implied that after studying the book the reader would have a superb memory for all occasions. Several weeks later our colleague told us how much he had enjoyed the book and how his memory had improved through using the techniques. Since the book had apparently served the purpose we asked for its return, only to be told by a shamefaced colleague: 'I'm awfully sorry but I cannot remember where I put it.' We still haven't got it back! Forget any attempt to train your memory but by all means learn those techniques which, when conscientiously applied, will help you to remember facts and figures.

One of the main reasons why we forget things so easily is that all too often we see but do not really *observe*. The story is told of a professor who was giving the first lecture of the year to a group of new medical students. 'Today I am going to teach you the most important lesson you will ever learn during your studies. Listen carefully. In front of me in these three glass beakers are samples of urine taken from three patients. These samples can tell us a great deal about the health of the patients. Although you need complicated equipment to do a full analysis you can, however, get a good idea from the colour, smell and taste.' Then to the horror of the students the professor dipped his finger into the samples one by one and they saw him put it to his lips. 'Now I want you to do the same.' Bravely each student looked, smelled and tasted each sample in turn. 'Now for that lesson I promised you. Not one of you noticed that I dipped *this* finger into the samples but licked *another one*. The important lesson you have all learned today is — OBSERVE.' And this is the lesson we give to you. If you want to remember anything, *observe* it.

There are three main ways in which the material that you study can be remembered and become part of your intellectual lore: by the use of *repetition, association*, and *memory-joggers* or *mnemonics*. Each causes you to observe what it is that you are trying to remember. The mnemonic for these three is RAM: *Repetition, Association, Mnemonics*. You will find that all of these will help, but perhaps one of them will have better results for you than the other two. Experiment until you find the techniques that are most effective in allowing you to recall what you have studied.

Repetition

This is the oldest technique in teaching. The chanting of arithmetical tables by the whole class, day after day, used to impress the data so firmly that none of the circumstances of later life could eliminate that early acquirement. But repetition need not be vocal, although the oral and vocal aspects of study are today not sufficiently used in colleges. Repetition can be visual; and we advocate this technique in the section on Notes of notes in chapter 4, and the section on Swot cards in chapter 7. See also the section on Review and recall in the present chapter.

Association

A registrar of an adult-education college was a master of the technique of association. His adult pupils would come, possibly at long intervals, to the courses in which they were interested, but he was seldom at a loss in remembering a name. 'How do you do it?' we asked. He was somewhat reluctant to explain, but finally did so, although if the associative method that he used had got to the ears of his victims, it might have been embarrassing. He did not attempt to remember all the features that together make up a face. Instead he remembered some single characteristic, usually derogatory! Ms L. walked with turned-out feet; Mr J. had a large bulbous red nose; Ms S. twittered like a sparrow. The unkind but graphic association of names with feet and noses and twittering conversation was enough to bring both to mind, and allowed the registrar to greet each student by name, even after a long interval. This may not work for you; try to find out how associations assist you. Don't hesitate to use them even if they sound silly or have to be kept private. For some months we had, at intervals, to remember the number 0661224. The association was 'Oh, two sixes are twelve'. The 24 was easy, since the two sixes led to the two twelves. Childish perhaps, but the number never had to be written down.

This is simply one illustration of the technique of association, but the technique is suitable for wider application. For example, suppose that for some reason you wish to remember a long list of dissociated objects such as aeroplane, alarm clock, carrot, television, etc. You associate in a ridiculous or exaggerated way aeroplane with alarm clock, alarm clock with carrot, carrot with television and so on. The more ridiculous you make the association the easier it will be to recall. It helps to make the visual association moving and in colour. To show how our minds work we would visualise an aeroplane tearing down the runway dragging alarm clocks behind it on strings. Then we would visualise an alarm clock with carrots for fingers and imagine that when the alarm goes off it switches on the television set. And . . . — but you try: why should we continue to make fools of ourselves! Seriously though, the method is very effective. We are not kidding you; it does work. Try for yourself: write down 20 disconnected articles and rapidly associate, as in the example above, each successive pair from beginning to end. You will, no doubt, be amazed to find that you can recite the list in order quite easily.

If you wish to extend your new-found talent try to remember the list in any order. To do this, number each article and associate each number with its own 'hook', for example, your list might begin as follows

Number	Hook	Article
1	bun	aeroplane
2	pew	clock
3	bee	carrot
4	core	television

This time you associate in a ridiculous way bun and aeroplane, pew and clock, bee and carrot and so on. If then someone asks you to name article 4, you simply think of the permanent hook for 4 (core) and a ridiculous picture of a set made of apple cores brings to mind television. Similarly with item 35 or any other. Of course there is no advantage in this method if you have to look up the hooks. Because the method is so useful — not only in this connection but also for other memory techniques — many years ago we committed to memory our own personal hooks for each number from 1 – 100. Whenever we have to remember lists for lectures, appointments or even shopping, we simply associate each item or idea on the list with the appropriate hook. The amazing thing about memory is that you can use the same hooks for a multitude of lists without ending up in confusion.

Knowing the hooks from 1 – 100 extends the possibilities enormously. You can remember standard facts and figures, dates, telephone numbers — in fact anything with numbers in it.

Suppose we wish to commit to memory the date of the fictitious Battle of the Big Bend in 1482. *Our* hooks for 14 and 82 are tyre and fan. Now imagine the scene with the soldiers camped on the banks of a big bend in a river. Over the hilltop come Indians riding on tyres. Instead of hatchets they have fans and as they pass through the soldiers' camp they hit the soldiers and say: 'There you are dead.' Silly? Maybe, but we defy any reader of this book to forget the scene, which then connects with the date of that battle. Such is the strength of association.

Another way of making associative links is by using the heading and sub-heading techniques of chapter 4, and especially by drawing the pattern diagram showing relationships between the facets of an aspect of study. If your memory is visual, as many are, the pattern diagram in chapter 4, if looked at frequently, will be remembered as a series of linked ideas emerging from a central theme. Here, you will have used both repetition and association — a powerful combination.

All that we have written in this section has been in a light vein, but there is a very serious side to it. The techniques can be adapted for use in your studies to great effect. Try them.

Mnemonics

These may often take the form of rhymes, which are more easily remembered than bare facts. The old school rhyme for the succession of English kings and queens is an example. The rhyme

> Willie, Willie, Harry, Stee,
> Harry, Dick, John, Harry three

(with many more immortal lines to follow) can be translated into the more dignified list: William I, William II, Henry I, Stephen, Henry II, Richard I, John, Henry III — and so on through the Plantagenets and Tudors.

It is doubtful whether you can devise rhyming mnemonics for every purpose, but memory-joggers can be produced from the initials of various groups of associated topics. For example, in chapter 4, the mnemonic CHIC is used as a reminder of what you need to do to write an attractive page of notes with punch. In this chapter we use MACRO as a mnemonic.

The mnemonic RAM reminds you of repetition, association and mnemonics, and these three techniques can be used in combination or separately to retain in your memory the facts, ideas or opinions that you encounter in your studies.

Do not merely stare at facts which you hope to remember, but see if you can devise a memory-jogger by arranging them so that the initials form another word which, perhaps, you associate with some experience in your life.

A: Aims of Study

In dealing with the techniques of studying, memory has been treated first, for without memory all study would be in vain. Notes that you can consult are of great value, but much of the fundamental interpretation of your subjects must be based on an effective memory when notes are not to hand. Assuming, then, that your memory of the principal facts of your subject, so far as you have studied it, is proving adequate, how can you improve the results of study by further techniques?

The principal mistake made by students in their studies is to place the aim or object of their work too far into the future. To some extent, this is engendered by the timing of college examinations, which occur only at long intervals. To set as your aim an examination seen only dimly at the end of a period of many months is to invite failure in your studies. The mountain of studies that must be mastered before that distant date assumes daunting

The mountain of studies which must be mastered assumes daunting proportions

proportions and you see nothing but a losing battle against time. Continuous assessment, which is used at many colleges in the United States, is more conducive to maintaining a short-term aim in the student's mind. His 'grade' rises and falls like a temperature chart as the weeks go by, according to his successes or failures in tests taken at short intervals.

In the absence of such continuous assessment, officially applied, you must make a serious attempt to produce the short-term aims within your own thinking. Instead of visualising as your ultimate goal an examination many months ahead, break the subject into many parts. Take as your aim the thorough understanding of that part being considered by your lecturer at the time you are studying. Do not wait for him to hand you the technique; you know what the title of the sub-topic is. Look it up in the six textbooks mentioned in chapter 4, draw a pattern diagram and study the rays or branches one by one, committing part to memory and part to short notes for further use. Eliminate from your mind the great sweep and span of the total subject. A wide view is essential in beginning study, but not in this context. Your learning must be a technique of building up knowledge in small doses, as articulated parts of a whole. The wider field, which of course must be your ultimate aim, will then be covered naturally without any special effort.

C: Concentration

Boswell quotes Samuel Johnson as saying, *'Depend upon it, Sir, when a man knows he is to be hanged in a fortnight it concentrates his mind wonderfully.'* If we replace 'hanged' by 'examined' the aphorism is still true, and even more apt than the original. Unfortunately, such a concentration only a fortnight before the examination — which is too often the accepted state of affairs — is quite useless as a means of understanding and learning the skills of the subject. With such little time for repetition and association, there is a very rapid loss of recall and a decay of memory. To rely solely on late revision has been proved quite ineffectual as a means of obtaining acceptable results in an examination.

Concentration during study is more important to your career than concentration in the course of a rugger match. Yet, when playing on the rugger field you concentrate effortlessly. Nothing comes between you and the action of the game. No thoughts intrude from outside; you are not 'upset' or 'disturbed' by external noises such as yells from the touchline. All your faculties are directed to a focus on the game in which you are an active participant. Yet, when it comes to concentrating on the work involved in training you for a career, the standard that you achieve is inferior. You are 'upset' and 'disturbed' by every extraneous circumstance. The buzzing of a fly or the noise of conversation in the corridor outside can divert your attention in an instant, and study fades into decline. This picture is one that we have often seen and is, believe us, very common.

Such lack of concentration, whether great or small, is a very serious matter. Unless your attention is encouraged to focus on what you are doing, and your mind is prevented from straying laterally, you will be working at low efficiency. Much less will be accomplished than you are capable of doing. Man works far below his capacity; some writers have put a figure on the deficiency but it is of little value to you to make quantitative estimates. It is sufficient to realise that you, and all your fellow men, are rarely at full stretch. You can accomplish much more without any damage to health or mental stability. Think of the motto of Gordonstoun School in Scotland — *Plus est en vous.*

The buzzing of a fly can divert your attention

You have more in you: all right, let's accept that. Why does it not come out? Why is your concentration so wavering? Why do you pick up the evening paper and linger over tales of local gossip or distress when you have important tasks to carry out? It is entirely tied up with the *intensity of interest or desire* which you apply to the various things you do. If your desire is strong and your interest intense, your concentration is also strong and intense. Your mind doesn't stray when you are playing the game to which your interest is anchored. Strong concentration is the key to effective study. You can then work closer to your real ability — twice or three times what you did before. With real concentration and with conscious techniques, carefully followed, you can free many more hours for the activity of educating yourself in the wide ambit of a college life — social, intellectual, argumentative and sportive — and so grow in personality. To release this time you must not tolerate desultory study, giving up at the slightest excuse before any solid result is accomplished.

Do not *try* to concentrate; that doesn't work. Try to develop an interest in what you are studying. *Interest* and *desire* are the keys to concentration and effective study. You cannot force or dragoon yourself into a concentrated effort. Only some over-riding interest in the subject (including an imposed pseudo-interest such as the imminence of an examination), or the desire brought to the forefront of your mind by a growing fascination in what you are reading, will finally shut out the rest of the world. Only then does your attention begin to focus.

For the development of concentration there is no need for absolute quiet, although silence is an added bonus. In your professional practice you may have to carry out important and complex work, such as the writing of a critical report, in the noise of a factory or with a bulldozer working outside the window of your office. Concentration allows you to 'switch off' your hearing so that, although the noise gives signals to the brain, it is not recognised as relevant to the purpose in hand, and does not register in the consciousness.

Lack of concentration is a serious handicap to a professional person, whether young or old. Work it out of your system so that, eventually, what you are doing becomes for the time being the only thing in existence. The popular habit of listening with half an ear to a radio during study is a deliberate division of attention. Some say that it helps them to study, but don't accept that. They have probably never achieved undivided concentration. Try experiments to find out how well you can eliminate outside influences, using all sorts of conditions until the technique is perfected. Try your concentration by studying on a seat in the park; go where street traffic is loud through the window; turn on a radio, turn it off. Find out how you can work at highest efficiency — it pays dividends.

To increase your interest in the subjects of your course may be difficult; some of them are pretty dull, and textbook writers often make them duller. One technique is to divert your approach away from merely absorbing what you are told in books or lecture notes, and try to write down, and answer, as many questions as you can about each page. What happens if . . . ? How far can this rule be applied? When were these statements first made? How does this work in practice? Some of the questions may not be very important; you find that out as you make the answers. But you will be treating the subject like some crossword puzzle, trying to link in the fabric and background.

Concentration comes from an interest in your subject

The important technique, which keeps you going as an automaton until interest and desire take over, and concentration sharpens to a fine point, is that of having a rigorous time-table of study laid down in advance. Motivation develops as you get the habit of work. You are all alone; no one will interfere; in a college no one helps your studies (although your best friend may do the opposite and interfere by dropping in for a chat). The time-table imposed *by you* as the coach, *on you* as the trainee, acts as a control device. The time-table is discussed at length in the section on Organisation of study.

To summarise, then, *concentration* is a skill you must develop if you are to work at high efficiency. The traditional 'absent mindedness' of a professor represents a concentration on some subject removed from the daily life going on around the poor old man. He is switched off, but concentrated in another sphere. Try a bit of 'absent mindedness' when studying. Concentration does not come from an effort of will; it does come from an *interest* in your subject.

R: Review and Recall

Recall is the ability to remember what you have learnt in education and training. It is almost another term for *memory*, but recall must be under control and should also be 'instant'. It is of little use to remember the answer to an examination question as you leave the room, or to say later with head in hands, 'But I knew it so well', surprised at your ability to remember it now but your inability to recall it at the time when you most needed it. You should not be surprised. It is your technique that is at fault — remedy it.

If there is one established fact about the techniques of learning, which has been proved beyond all possible doubt, it is that what you have studied decays rapidly from the memory unless it is frequently reviewed. This is merely another way of reminding you of the technique of *repetition* examined in the section on Memory. If you make reviews or revision on a pre-conceived plan, you will have, eventually, instant recall.

Too many students imagine that all they need do is to note down and read over the contents of lectures, and then to have a quick revision before the examination. It would be as sensible to take one run round the football field, look casually at the book of rules, and then wait happily at home until the day of the match, expecting that you will score a winning goal before enthusiastic supporters. You can imagine what 'support' you would get, and what the coach would say to such a programme. At most colleges of higher education you are, unfortunately, your own study coach. Control and instruct your trainee, who is *you*.

Review consists of making yourself familiar with the section of knowledge concerned, by re-reading notes and books, by exercises (particularly if the work is numerical or mathematical) and by oral discussion and written comment. Reviews are the training sessions of your academic work and should be as frequent as the work-outs for a team. The necessary frequency is known. It has been established that new information rapidly decays from the memory; it cannot be kept ready for instant recall unless its impression on the brain is renewed. The period between renewals may gradually be extended but, to begin with, it must be short. The first review must take place within 24 hours, and preferably within 12 hours if you are not to spend a lot of time later in resurrecting the item and trying to remember it. The second review should be the following day, and then a slight relaxation can be allowed, with two days and four days elapsing. However, if recall is then not found to be effective, the review periods must be brought closer together again. There can be no relaxation in reviewing, which should be continued by means of a precise programme until the work is well known. Even then, further reviews are valuable, for *over-learning,* that is, making reviews after the work is easily recalled, is a sound method of establishing it without fear of serious decay of recall.

Think of all the new material coming to your notice in various classes and from other sources, and remember that all of this should be reviewed throughout the whole period of study — the term or the session. You can understand the need for a programme, constructed in advance and regarded by you as legally binding on your attention. In the section on Organisation of study, this matter is brought to a head.

One of the interesting things about college studies is the dumbness of the student — using the word in its accurate sense and not as sometimes applied rudely to blondes! Listening to lectures means silence on your part; study is also silent; the library maintains silence; you say no word at an examination. Yet the early development of ideas was done orally. The philosophers debated; St Paul was taken to speak at the Areopagus in Athens 'for all the Athenians and strangers which were there spent their time in nothing else, but either to tell, or to hear some new thing'; the House of Commons clears the ground for legislation by public discussion; and the speakers in Hyde Park orate. Yet in college the amount of oral review of studies is minimal. Each week you ought to have a regular session with a couple of your friends, for a discussion review (behind closed doors) of some part of your studies agreed in advance. Don't get on to politics!

O: Organisation of Study

If you know what your aims are; if you make sure that you know how to memorise and recall; if your reviews are effective, with good concentration, you may feel yourself well on the way to becoming a successful student with a bright future. But take warning. Effective study does not flower by chance even if all these aspects are covered. MACR does not form a word that can be Used as mnemonic, and *Memory, Aims, Concentration* and *Review* still lack one thing. That is *Organisation,* bringing the mnemonic to its final state: MACRO. We wish your studies to result in success, but such a result is never fortuitous. Planning is essential.

The yawning attitude — 'Well, I must go and do some work, I suppose' — can bring down students with good innate ability, while a steady and properly constructed programme can allow those with only mediocre skill to maintain an excellent standard, and to have more free and unencumbered time for the social and sporting facets of a full college life. The degree finally obtained when study is organised is a credit as much to organisational ability as to brilliance. As we mention in the section on Concentration, a good time-table of study can take the place of motivation until such motivation develops of its own accord. Then the time-table may take another role — that of curbing the tendency to study only those subjects with the greatest appeal.

Hours in a Week

The number of hours in a week is 168. When allowance is made for the hours needed for sleep and eating and keeping fit and carrying out Union and Society activities, you would be pardoned for thinking that there are not many left to be used for organising a study programme. We challenge you to do an experiment. Over the next week (assuming it to be typical) keep a note of exactly what you do with your time each day. Make a balance sheet. The income is 168 hours and remember you cannot increase this even in times of severe inflation — you have all the time there is. There is no use going on strike for more. The expenditure is the time you use for everything except private study. Your answer will probably be something like this

	Expenditure	*Income*	
Sleep 8 hours/day	56		
Eating 3 hours/day	21		
Travel 2 hours/day	10		
Classes	25		
Recreation & sport	20		
	132	168	Balance 36 hours

Bearing in mind that we have already allowed for sleeping, eating and formal classes in the full week, the balance represents 4½ working days at 8 hours per day, available for private study. Amazing, isn't it? Where does all the time go to? Well, if we had been a little more realistic, we would have included another item in the expenditure side — *wasted time*, which some of you may have included under the heading private study! The point of this simple experiment is to show you that although there are only 168 hours in a week there is ample time for private study *provided you are prepared to organise your life*. It is so easy to fritter away time.

Making a Time-table

One approach to organising your time is to start with the 'contact hours' in college, when you are usually being introduced to something new. If the new work is given to you in a lecture, you can assume that you require two hours of study for each hour of lecture — for reading of the subject before the lecture, and as a first review (within the first 24 hours). If the work is presented in a laboratory class, it is best to make the necessary studies and the first draft writing-up of the report immediatcly after the laboratory work, before you leave the lab. This keeps everything fresh in your mind until you finally explain it in writing, and also leaves the evenings free for study. Students who spend many hours writing up laboratory reports in the evenings have not organised their time effectively. Try using the end of the lab time and 'free periods' during the week. Ideally, the evening study periods should be used for reviews of the work given in lectures, and the daily 'free periods' for writing up practical work.

Nothing ever works out as ideal, but let us assume for the sake of demonstration that you can deal with much of the course work during the day, so that your evenings are free for work on the lecture and seminar periods. Suppose, then, that you can allow the equivalent of four hours each evening for six days a week. This 24 hours is only two-thirds of the 36 hours available; it should be considered a minimum time to allocate to private study. You must work out your personal pattern so as to suit your individual conditions. The time of 24 hours might be split into, say, 20 hours for new material and four hours for reviews of past material or 18 hours and six hours. This is not a superabundance of time but, *used effectively,* it will be just adequate and will allow for about 10 lectures a week. If your programme is like many we have seen, you will probably have more than 10 lectures per week, and you will have to work with greater efficiency and use more of the available 36 hours.

These ideas show you how you can start on sketching out a programme. In the next phase, list the number of subjects and the days of the week on which you have lectures on these topics. Then look through your diary, marking off times when you have meetings or recreational engagements. These are allowed for in the balance sheet and are part of your education. Then, decide on the times you are going to work in your room. For example in the evenings you might consider 7 to 9 (too little), 7 to 11, or 6 to 12 (too much). Having decided on this, map out a very careful schedule of subject studies for every day (or equivalent periods at weekends) during the term. Check the section on Reading effectively, and also remember the idea of having a debate on a chosen topic for say half an hour once a week so that you can use your voice and express your ideas and opinions. The lecturer will not be there and so you will be free to be rude if you want to be.

Some principles to be kept in mind are given, with arguments, in the section on Reading effectively, but here we can note the final results.

(1) Do not study for an extended period on one subject. One period might contain three or even four subjects.

(2) Do not study consecutively subjects that are similar. For example, one mathematical subject should not be followed by another.

(3) Work strictly to the clock, and have definite rest periods between topics. Study for 50 minutes and have 10 minutes

complete break. This is a dangerous but necessary technique. It is necessary for the efficiency of study, but dangerous in that you may let the ten minutes drift on into the next study period. You are your own coach: look after the training of your favourite trainee!

(4)   Always start a period on a particular topic with a review of that day's lecture. The rest of the 50 minutes should be used to look back on the previous lectures and notes on the same topic. Further notes should be made during reviewing, so that you are not merely a passive recipient of information. Ask yourself questions.

(5)   In each subject, have a short-term goal. You are to make yourself the master of a particular sub-topic or sub-sub-topic rather than prepare for the year's examination in the whole subject. As the sub-topics mount up, mark them off on the pattern diagram (see figure 2 in chapter 4).

(6)   Have as much activity as possible: work through problems; discuss orally with friends once a week; write notes. Do not think that you can learn by sitting back with your feet up reading a book.

(7)   Elaborate your notes; have coloured pencils ready for underlining. Give the pages of notes an open and individual pattern. Mark your textbooks to a pre-conceived plan. This is one reason for not relying too much on library books. A marked book is much more useful than one that has merely been read and is therefore without marks and comments in the margins.

You should know weeks ahead just what you are to be studying and at what time. Of course, all programmes may creak and require alteration as the term moves on, but do make a programme in diary form or on a bar chart, or both. The bar chart, built up as you go, shows you how you are keeping up to programme — and teaches you about the idiosyncrasies of bar charts!

The time-table must: (a) be written down in detail and (b) be adhered to strictly. In our experience, those students who work to a study time-table never fail to attain the standard expected by the examiners — it is not a very demanding one. The attainment of a good standard depends on programmed progress sustained through the term from beginning to end. Examination success becomes a by-product of controlled study.

Reading Effectively

Of the methods scrutinised in this book, *studying* is one of the most impersonal. The communication, to a large extent, is by means of the printed word. There is also, in the fabric of the study method, the personal communication from you to yourself in the form of notes. Notes are so often hard to understand, even for the person who wrote them, and yet they should be the most transparently clear of all means of communication. You wrote them; you read them; you know what you like to find in the written or printed word. Your notes are personal to you. Why then do students often find their own notes so strangely uncommunicative? Read chapter 4 and act on it.

Leaving notes aside for the present, how should you approach the printed word? What techniques will distil from the words the essence of what the author is trying to say? Authors often write, curiously enough, for themselves. Asked why he wrote a book that few are buying, an author will say: 'I simply had to get it out of my system.' This is surely the antithesis of communication. Textbooks that are helpful and communicative reach that standard because the author had in his mind the reader with whom he wished to communicate. If he had not had this picture in his mind, he might inadvertently have written in a way that tried to satisfy different types of individual in the same book. This situation has occurred in our experience. Make sure that the textbook you pick up and use is written for *you*.

Chapter 5, on the use of the library, is an anti-browsing chapter. We show you how to use the library without mooning along the shelves, but by using the index and other efficient methods of communication. However, there is a time for intelligent browsing, especially in bookshops and sometimes in the library also. This browsing can give you a broad view of the subject you are studying. In the bookshops you can have your finger on the pulse of today's publishing world in your subject. The bookseller is there to sell books; those on his shelves are, therefore, attractive to the reading public in that topic and are worth exploring. Look for the textbooks that speak to you in clear terms. For example, hold one sub-topic in mind and look that up in each of the texts, comparing the treatments. If the selected topic is clearly described to you in a particular book, the other topics are likely to be equally attractive.

Your Personal Library

In an impersonal means of communication such as studying, every aid that you can find is required; it is required at your elbow and not in some distant place. You *must* build up a small library of your own: one or two books will not be enough; you should, ideally, have at least two on each topic. Your college or lecturers may have provided you with a selected list. If they haven't, ask them. This is one of the actions in which you must train your lecturers (see chapter 3).

Dr Peter Mann, Reader in Sociology in the University of Sheffield, conducted a survey among undergraduates on the use of book lists, libraries and bookshops, and on how much was spent on the purchase of books. The results were both surprising and depressing. Fewer than half of the undergraduates reported receiving reading lists from all or most of their lecturers. About one student in seven never used a library at all. More than a third of the undergraduates never ordered books at the university bookshops, and less than a third of the grant provided by the Department of Education and Science was spent as it was supposed to be. Dr Mann concluded that students are uninstructed in the use of books, and laid the blame on the lecturers. Would you not be highly suspicious of the mechanic who services your car, if you found that he did not buy or borrow his most important tools, did not know how to use them, never looked into a tool-shop window and had had no instruction in the use of the tools from the foreman? If your lecturer has not given you a book list, get one of your larger colleagues to persuade him to do so.

Students often object to the expense of textbooks, but remember that all your friends will be trying to borrow the best textbooks from the college library. Undergraduate textbooks may be in the library index, but they are seldom on the shelves for borrowing. If the subject is a 'classical' one — one that changes little and is of long standing — you may find old editions of early textbooks on the library shelves but, if the subject is a developing one, you haven't a hope of borrowing the right texts, because they are all out on loan: give up the idea. Anyway, you require the book for long periods, which a library seldom allows.

Remember that you have denied yourself the possibility of making an income for at least three years. Add up that loss and ask yourself whether a few more pounds spent on books to prosecute the purpose that brought you to college will, in later years, make any difference to your funds. (For the present you may have to give up smoking, but that could be an excellent idea in itself!) We want you to be efficient in your studies. To achieve this you must buy textbooks, for otherwise all the effort that we have expended in writing this book for your benefit will have been wasted and *we* don't like wasting effort. If you are to get the best from our book, you must keep buying other people's books also, and hoard them as a precious collection. Put your name on an inner page as well as on the fly-leaf and don't lend them. Of course, we hope that you will not just browse through our book in a bookshop, as you may well be doing now, but will buy and use it! It will pay you dividends, so long as you don't say 'Silly old codgers' and put it on a top shelf.

Remember that textbooks serve as reference books for many years after you have 'mastered' the subject. Don't sell yours in any second-hand dealing in the Union. We frequently consult both old and new textbooks on our shelves to check some small point.

Marking Textbooks

One of the reasons for owning rather than borrowing textbooks is that they need to be marked to get the best out of them. A textbook without fingerprints and pencil marks is like a spade unsoiled by digging. In your studies, when you want to refer to information about a given point, you have two methods. You can consult the index of the book, which will give you the page number required. This is the best method in the early days; never thumb through a textbook hoping that the point you want to study will leap out at you. It won't, and this procedure wastes time. Use the index, but have a second line of attack ready — mark lines and paragraphs in the textbook for future reference.

Retain the books; they will be of use to you long after the degree has been awarded

As you become more familiar with the subject, after repeated reviews, data can be found and appreciated if you have made the pages of your textbooks as individual and readily recognisable as the pages of your notes. This is done by highlighting and emphasising the rather amorphous print by means of colour marking. Codes can easily be devised to suit your individual tastes, but the following are a few hints on which you might build.

(1) An important printed heading for a wide topic (one for which you might draw a pattern diagram) can be ringed, or outlined by a rectangle of red lines.

(2) Within this main heading, the links of the pattern diagram when they appear in the text could have an underline in red. There are nearly 20 of these links in the pattern diagram shown as an example in chapter 4 (see figure 2).

(3) Sub-sub-headings might have an underline in blue, or perhaps a dotted underline.

(4) Sentences that you think might be illuminating in later study might be underlined in green. Not only does this pick them out, but the underline can be used only for the main emphasis of the sentence. By leaving the adjectival clauses and parenthetical qualifications without underlines, the main parts of the sentence can be read as a single punch line.

(5) You can run a line down the edge of a paragraph that you think you may wish to emphasise. This can be done in soft black pencil. Lines down one or both edges of the paragraph are somewhat less overpowering than underlines, and carry a different meaning.

(6) Dotted instead of full lines give another range of meaning if you want to sub-divide as far as that.

(7) Finally, you ought to accustom yourself to writing cross-references to the same or allied topics in the margins of the textbooks. The references can be to other parts of the same book, to another textbook or to your own Shelfold notes (see chapter 4).

Underlining is the recognised and usual method of marking texts in books or printed papers but, if you wish to be up-to-date, we recommend that you try *highlighting* instead. This consists of marking the key word or phrase that you wish to emphasise with a felt marker pen. These highlighting pens use transparent ink so that the text can be read through the coloured line, which extends over the whole depth of the type. The colours are bright and are called *fluorescent* to distinguish them from the normal opaque colours in the usual felt-tip pens. For example, the key words of a pattern diagram, as they occur in the text, could be highlighted, and all the recommendations on underlining can also be followed by highlighting.

Activity

In developing study techniques it is difficult to produce anything approaching activity. Students lie back in chairs with feet on the table or stretched towards the electric fire, and drift passively through the textbook. This may be an acceptable technique for reading science fiction or a romantic novel, but for the study of important texts it is not only inappropriate, but also damaging to study and uneconomic of time. Marking texts and comparing one textbook with another are active techniques, and in study it is active techniques that produce the desired results. If you read again the sections covered by the mnemonic MACRO, you will appreciate that the best effects are produced when you do not merely soak up the words of the textbook author, like some print-absorbing sponge. You must prod him with coloured pencils, or tell him he must be joking when he makes heavy weather of something that another author does neatly. Never accept; always challenge the author; put question marks in the margin when you don't believe him. You may be wrong, but you have been active. Activity must be on your part and not on the part of the authors you are reading. By such challenges you will learn to challenge and be critical of your own judgements and writings.

The Use of Your Notes

Another active task during your reading programme is to compare your lecture notes with the textbook study of the subject. If you have made your notes properly (for 'making' rather than 'taking' is the appropriate term for most lecture notes), the pages will contain the *key words* recommended in chapter 4, a few brief references to standard work with plenty of space left and the final conclusion clearly written in the right-hand margin. Short notes here and there will indicate the path that the lecturer has taken through the study, but words will be few and blank spaces many. After all, the paper has not cost you anything: your girl-friend has encouraged her boss to look for blank A4 pages for the impecunious student; or, girls, your boy-friend works in an office where his wastepaper basket would be full of the stuff if he did not remember your need.

Now comes the use of the blank spaces. Derivations and proofs can be written in, with your full understanding. You already understood the derivation in class, for you were looking at the blackboard and did not obscure your attention by scribbling down everything. You are not at a loss and can choose, from the textbooks to hand, the derivation that looks best, or that is closest to that of the lecturer. You might even find that the lecturer's blackboard work was straight out of a textbook, perhaps one that he has written himself. There is nothing underhand or suspicious about this. It merely means that he has selected the best presentation of the subject for your assistance. If, of course, you spend the lecture period with your nose in a notebook trying to take everything down instead of *understanding*, you may well be confused when you come to study (see chapter 3).

Other comments (from other authors) that you find interesting and that look as if they might be useful can go down in the blank spaces. An equally acceptable technique is to write in the blank spaces the reference to a textbook that you may like to consult later. It is simpler to make the note 'Jones p. 253' than to write down a long dissertation which is already in print. Later, your active reference to page 253 will be a review of some fact you need to know, and an improvement of memory. After all, Jones spent a long time getting the wording right, and you won't be able to improve on it. Also, you have paid Jones (in buying the book) for the right to read and mark his communication.

There is far too little reciprocal traffic between textbooks and Shelfolds (see chapter 4). Mark the margins of textbooks with references to Shelfolds. If notes are well written they are as good as any textbook, and much more personal to you. But you cannot understand or study a subject from notes alone, as too many students try to do.

All this marking and writing and reference back and forth between different textbooks and notes is the correct way to deal with impersonal communication of the kind that you encounter in your studies. Between you, your notes and your textbooks there must be a three-way traffic. Activity in study develops concentration through review and interest, and the efficiency of study rises dramatically. And you don't fall asleep, as you are inclined to do if you try to be an absorbent sponge, soaking in what the authors say as if they had the last word. *You* have the last word; it is your study.

Reading Periodicals

Every college spends large sums on periodicals, proceedings of societies and institutions and research papers of all kinds. These are intended chiefly for the research worker, but undergraduates will find the periodicals referring to their particular interest of increasing value as the course progresses. The periodicals keep you in touch with what is going on in practice and indicate new developments in research. Set aside at least half-an-hour each week to study a selected number (don't try to read them all) of periodicals in the college Periodicals Room. Keep to the same three or four each week. The effort will be well worth while and you will realise that you are not merely a 'student' in the lay understanding of the term, but a professional person with a place in society. Don't avoid the Periodicals Room.

Think and Act

Think (A): Viewpoint

Study, if it is to be effective, must be active and critical and not passive. It must be continuous from the start of the course. It is based on textbooks and papers and on well-made personal notes.

Think (B): Techniques

Like other aspects of communication, study depends on well-applied and well-understood techniques. These are based on memory and recall; concentration; frequent reviews; organisation of study time; effective reading.

Act (C): Your Personal Library

Build a personal library: a collection of books and papers. Purchase of books must be followed by careful reading and marking. Do not read from beginning to end but use the books as reference texts. Retain the books; they will be of use long after the degree has been awarded.

Act (D): Active Cross-reference

References to other books, to technical papers, to periodicals and to your own personal notes must appear in the margins of the books in your own library. In this way an active reciprocal flow takes place between your thinking and that of those authors whose work you accept as of value.

3
Listening to Lectures

You have to accept the lecturers you find in the college you attend — hardly an original thought but nevertheless an illuminating and sobering one. In the time you have at college, you cannot alter them. Any time you spend on agitating about the system of teaching or lecturing is time altruistically spent, for it will benefit only your successors. It takes at least three years to put into effect any major alteration in a course, and by that time you will have left college, we hope, with a completed degree. So don't grumble about your lecturers; learn how to train them. Many of them certainly need a good deal of instruction in the art of lecturing. This deficiency is recognised, not only by you but by the body of lecturers themselves and by the college authorities. Courses, seminars and discussions are held at intervals within an individual college or within a broader catchment in order to improve college teaching. Deficiencies are there but you can counteract them to your personal advantage. This book deals only with *your* tasks in communication, and not with those of the lecturer; *he* needs another volume.

Remember that a lecturer is usually appointed, not because he can teach, but because he knows a great deal about a particular topic in which he has specialised. His chief function is not to teach as a schoolmaster teaches, but to keep abreast of thought and development in his subject — by reading, by research into new aspects, by meeting and corresponding with other specialists, by attending conferences, by travel and often by solving real-life problems affecting people outside the college. He is then expected to transmit to you not merely the dry bones of well-accepted knowledge, but the living and growing body of his experience. What he tells you should be the distilled essence of what he has personally found. You may snort and think that this is very far-fetched but you can be assured that the majority of lecturers who appear before you not only know their subjects but are enthusiastic about them and about transmitting their knowledge to you. Otherwise, they would not be lecturing in a college but pursuing some more lucrative occupation!

On the other hand, if your lecturer is apparently unsuccessful at the job of transmitting his knowledge and enthusiasm to you, it may be you, the student, who is at fault. You may not be applying the *techniques* necessary to take advantage of this opportunity of obtaining wisdom as well as information. The lecturer is a mine of illumination, and of the philosophy and criticism of his subject, but *you* must do the digging.

Remember: the lecturer is not there to teach you. You are there to learn. Nobody else can learn on your behalf. It is doubtful whether the term 'teaching' can be strictly applied much beyond the primary school. It certainly does not apply in tertiary education in colleges. No teaching is possible without the co-operation of the students who are supposed to be learning. Here is a true example of this. A student at one of our universities was taking part in one of those unproductive confrontations between students and senior members of the university. The belligerent young man, in comment on some discussion about teaching, glared furiously at the senior member and shouted: *All right then; go ahead; teach me something'*. When exaggerated to this degree, it is evident that neither teaching nor learning could ensue, for co-operation was absent and opposition in full force. No amount of lecturing can produce any advance in your knowledge unless you have the will and the wish to learn, and know what a lecture is meant to achieve. You, not the lecturer, must learn to accomplish the desired result. The onus is on *you*.

Alternatives to Lectures

There are alternatives to what is called 'the lecture system' — hardly an apt name, since anything less systematic or coherent than the uses made of a college lecture would be hard to find. Let us clear the alternatives out of the way; while they are often brought into discussions on the best methods of sharing knowledge with undergraduates, they have but limited scope, and there is no doubt that you must learn to handle lectures as the first step towards a fruitful co-operation with the staff at your college.

There are undoubtedly great advantages to the student if a staff member transmits his ideas and experience to only a few individuals at a time in a *tutorial* session. It is still used for the more advanced undergraduate work and for sharing knowledge gained in research. For general undergraduate studies, however, the tutorial has in most colleges been superseded by the lecture.

Other possibilities are *colloquia* or *seminars*. In these meetings, students come together to discuss a defined topic, whose main points are put forward by one of their own number; the staff members who attend do so not to teach but to play a part in guiding the discussion. This alternative to the lecture is probably the most rewarding method of sharing knowledge, but it demands a much greater enthusiasm and interest by the student. For those who attend merely because they are required to do so, rather than from a genuine interest, the seminar can be a waste of time. However, as for small group tutorials, colloquia and seminars are usually held only for the senior years of the course.

For the younger student, then, the main contact with senior members of the college is almost certainly through the lecture. If you can learn how to handle the lecture you will have little difficulty when you come to meet seminars.

The Number of Lectures

The more a lecturer is allowed to devise his own course and take an individualistic approach to his subject, the more valuable will be his contribution. Such freedom, however, often results in an overloading of the student's timetable. Each lecturer tends to look on his subject as of paramount importance. Similarly, in some subjects, the whole course is designed so that too many lectures are chasing too little study time. In such circumstances, knowledge of the techniques described in this chapter is of even greater importance to you, if you are to succeed in extracting value from lectures, and still have adequate time for private study.

Many college curricula, especially in scientific and technological subjects, subject the student to such a barrage of facts and opinions that he has little chance to pause and assess what has taken place so far. This lack of free time is one of the unfortunate and regrettable aspects of college life that some students have to experience. You can protest about this if it becomes a burden, but the time expended in doing so is probably inefficiently spent. See the discussion on the hours in a week in chapter 2.

When time is restricted it is more important than ever that you have a routine of work. In that routine, the ordered manipulation of facts and opinions presented in a lecture takes a high place. The greater the number of lectures you must attend, the tighter and more automatic must be your techniques, or else you will find after a week or two that you have only a mass of undigested scribbles as the poor product of the many lectures you have attended.

The Function of the Lecture

A college lecture is usually one of a series that ostensibly covers a syllabus, printed in the college prospectus (although perhaps in an abbreviated form). Some lecturers — from inclination or a sense of duty — follow the syllabus closely. Others may diverge into recent developments of part of the subject and leave you to read the well-established sections. Whatever the lecturer's technique, start your course by writing out a title-page summary of what the syllabus lists. Leave plenty of space between the topics mentioned in the printed syllabus and then find, in several textbooks, all of the possible subsidiary titles within each main topic. Some of these may be outside the scope of the particular class, but this you will discover later. Your main object is to have the whole scheme laid out before you on a single page. At some convenient time, take this to the lecturer — who will be flattered by your interest — and he can delete some and add other sub-divisions. Note that this should be done *before* the series of lectures commences, so that a mental map of the topic is before you when you attend the first lecture. Then apply the techniques relating to key words described in chapter 4.

Do not imagine, however, that lectures will always be held in the order shown in the syllabus or even that they will cover every aspect of it. The more original and individual the mind of the lecturer, the more valuable is what he says, but the less likely is he to be bound tightly by the syllabus. You are required to know the syllabus from your studies, but the lecturer need not lecture 'at' you on its every aspect. He is there to guide your learning process, which should be continually progressing. With his knowledge of the subject and his experience of guiding generations of students, the lecturer knows which aspects cause mental confusion and doubt, and which are readily understood by all students. If he is wise, he need not deal with the latter in his guiding lectures, but will merely refer to books in which these simpler topics are well set out.

The Function of the Student in the Lecture Period

Too many students look on lectures as mental filling-stations. They come with minds as empty as their notebooks, knowing little or nothing about the subject. They expect the lecturer to fill both mind and notebook with undeniable facts, which can then be regurgitated at examinations in a depraved and bowdlerised state. This is a travesty and a very sad experience for any lecturer. As he looks at examination papers undistinguished by any spark of originality, and recognises the pale image of his carefully prepared arguments, he finds, incongruously, that he is thinking of casting pearls!

Many students look on lectures as mental filling-stations

What then is the function of the student in the lecture period, if it is not to fill a notebook with what is written on the blackboard? The first thing to remember is that you are a *student* — that is, one who studies. This is the basis of your life; there is no such thing as teaching in the sense of having knowledge injected into you. The level of college education is too high for that simple idea. The lecture, then, can be no more than a guide to assist your studies. There is no chance of finally learning anything during a lecture, but there is a good chance that difficulties encountered in the study can be illuminated. But how can difficulties be assisted or cleared out of the way if, when attending the lecture, you know nothing of the topic discussed? The paradox is that, to receive help in understanding your subject, you must already know something about it.

We are forced, then, to the apparently bizarre idea that study of any aspect of the subject should precede as well as follow the lecture on it. This may seem idiotic to you, if you were brought up in the 'filling-station' tradition. But consider some sport — say, rock climbing. If you attend a mountaineering club lecture in order to discover whether you should attempt this sport, you will follow the discussion much more easily if you have read a little about it. In fact, we doubt whether you would go to such a lecture, dealing with a topic that has a fascination for you, without some preparation. You would have read of the exploits of some famous rock climber and you would be familiar with the meanings of such terms as abseiling, etrier, carabiner, piton and so on. Without such basic knowledge, you might gain some small insight into the sport, but at a much lower level of appreciation than if you had done some reading in advance. The same argument applies to your college subjects, and to a more important degree.

To be effective for you, the lecture should cover topics that you have already studied — if only briefly. You should at least have 'run over' the topic in textbooks before attending the lecture. Many lecturers (who are seldom trained educationalists) do not realise the importance of this statement, and announce their topics only when they appear at the lectern. *Such a situation should not be accepted; it must be changed in your own interests.* Ask the lecturer if he can possibly forecast what, at least, his next lecture is to contain. He might be willing to mention, in advance, at least some of the sub-topics he will deal with in the next couple of weeks. If your lecturer forgets, remind him politely. The value of the lecture is doubled or trebled if you have read — even in a desultory fashion, without making notes — the essential features of the forthcoming discussion. We have never found it an imposition to provide, at the beginning of a term a sheet of paper for each lecture setting out pre-requisite knowledge, the subject of the lecture and reference to textbook work which would probably not be treated except by a mention.

If your lecturer forgets, remind him politely

Bookwork

For a detailed discussion of how to make notes at lectures, see chapter 4. There is, however, one aspect of note-making in technical lectures that deserves attention here. In this circumstance, the term note-*taking* is more appropriate, for there is little creation or understanding in the process. The problem concerns what is usually known as *bookwork* — the arguments laying the basis of some subject in logical terms, and developing it to a proved law or relationship.

When this part of the subject appears, some 'lecturers' are almost silent, which is surely the ultimate in antithesis. They write on the blackboard steadily, with perhaps only an occasional brief explanation, developing the classical derivation of some fundamental relationship necessary to the understanding of the subject. This is 'taken down' by the students as if it were some original and astounding promulgation, no item of which had been heard before. In fact, the whole thing is certain to be fully explained in many textbooks, for there is nothing in an undergraduate course which has not had the attention of textbook writers. If you are in a very senior class you may, of course, be introduced to new research material, but the presentation will then be quite different.

When bookwork is laboriously copied, the opportunity is missed of clearing up difficult parts, and of allowing the student to *understand*. He is so busy copying that he does not appreciate such short comments as the lecturer may make, from time to time, to explain why a step is being taken. Lack of attention to explanations arises because the student is behind in his copying. It is easier for the lecturer to write than for the student to look at a distant blackboard and then back to his so-called 'notes', and so a phase difference develops between the blackboard and the class. We have even seen lecturers complete their lectures and leave the room while the students have had to sit for another few minutes taking down the last load from the blackboard!

This condition ought to be seen by all to be quite ridiculous and unacceptable, but it is all too common. It arises from the failure of the lecturer to tell the class in advance what he is to discuss and from the student thus being unable to read in advance the relevant pages in the textbooks. The lecturer's task is not to act in the mediaeval sense and be a reader of scarce books, but to explain the difficult parts of an abstruse subject. Books are not scarce even if they are somewhat costly. Detailed arguments, clearly printed, need not be re-written by the student during a lecture in a rushed and garbled fashion. Understanding is not present and time is wasted.

When this sort of presentation takes place, resist the inclination to bend over your notebook, except for jotting down a few key words. Sit back, listen and *understand*. Butt in with questions — you can be sure that your fellows are too busy scribbling even to notice that a question is needed. Then, when you return to your own room, you can look up the relevant pages and study them in the light of the explanations you have had.

Preferably, you should have been able to read the text over *before* the lecture. If you have not trained your lecturer to give you the information to which you are entitled — that he is to deal with such and such a topic on specific days — then get started with a process of attrition, backed by your friends, until he does produce a programme for the term.

Think and Act

Think (A): Viewpoint

A lecture is not a mental filling-station. Lectures are meant to stimulate study. Lecturers are not teachers. Lecturers in college are guides and advisers on the subjects of study.

Think (B): Attitude at Lectures

Concentrate and listen. Try to understand. Resist the urge to write continuously because others are doing so. Write key words; leave plenty of blank space.

Act (C): Training Lecturers

There are three vital programmes in which you must train your lecturers if they are to be the advisers and guides that they are supposed to be. Get them
  (a)   to supply you with book lists and reading lists
  (b)   to give you a dated list of topics to be discussed, so that you can study them *before* the date on which they will be treated
  (c)   to become accustomed to questions from the class.

Act (D): Studying Ahead

Learn to study ahead of the lectures by using the techniques of chapter 4 in the section on Key words and Pattern of notes and by drawing pattern diagrams for two topics soon to come up in the lecture programme. See how much more comprehensible and interesting the lectures become.

4
Making Notes

From the moment that you arrive at college you will be involved in what is popularly known as 'taking notes' and as likely as not within a few weeks you will be the possesser of tattered notebooks filled with illegible hieroglyphics or, worse still, of masses of mixed-up bits of paper.

Unfortunately, students are given little instruction on the techniques of making notes. This skill is assumed to be inborn and intuitive, but one glance at a student's notes shows this assumption to be unfounded. You have to learn how to make good notes — this is what this chapter is about. Follow our guidance and with a little practice you will find your notes transformed into a neat, annotated system of stored information that is readily available for retrieval when wanted. Incidentally, from now on the emphasis must be on *making* not *taking*. Students are expected to create their own notes: it is hard work and involves a craft skill as demanding as that required for oil paintings or pottery.

Why Do You Make Notes?

The purpose of making notes is primarily to set out, in a shortened but logical form, information that you have gathered from a variety of sources on a particular topic so that it can be used for revision purposes and as an aid to memory. As a secondary benefit, note-making helps to keep the mind active and alert and assists the learning process.

Organisation of Your Knowledge

When you think of a subject that you have been studying, do you know which part of it is of greatest importance? Do you know the bases of fact on which arguments depend? Can you place in relative importance the subsidiary aspects of the topic? These and other similar questions can be answered from the emphases placed in your finished body of notes. Notes, when well made, can provide a method of controlling and marshalling the mass of facts, opinions and proofs poured over you by your contact with other minds in lectures, reading and discussions. If your notes are not carefully made, with attention to the techniques that we propose, your knowledge will be unorganised and to that extent ineffective.

Supplementation of Print

The making of notes should be avoided when it is not necessary. There is no need to write copious notes that repeat what is clearly and carefully published in print. On the other hand, notes can supplement print by bringing together statements and opinions from diverse sources, in a brief and skeletal form. References to where the original and wider statement can be found should also be recorded. In this way the diverse opinions and findings of a topic are high-lighted and impressed on your consciousness, as a supplement to the printed textbooks that should be your guides. Notes on a topic by themselves are only of minor value unless they are backed up by wider statements, especially in a subject where there are controversies and differences of opinion.

Recall of Ideas and Facts

Recall is what fails to happen when you are stumped by an examination question. Later you will grunt in exasperated tones: 'But I knew it so well!' You may be quite right. The memory was there, and recall at leisure might have been possible if your study techniques were good. But when it is a question of instant recall, your notes must be compiled to act as a memory-trigger for the more important facts.

How to Store Notes

Before you study how to make notes, you must decide on a system of storage that is simple and gives ready access to what has been written. You should build your plan around A4 paper — the standard size. What then is the most efficient way of doing this? We can say categorically that the traditional

You take only one loose-leaf binder to lectures

students' bound notebook is quite inappropriate and furthermore costly. The only good use for such a notebook is for rough note-taking during laboratory experiments, so that you have all the data and observations before you when you come to write your report. This ensures that you do not lose observations made during a costly experiment. Otherwise forget the idea of a bound notebook.

The best method for notes is undoubtedly some loose-leaf system, preferably one using cords to hold the paper. The pages lie out flat on the desk when the cords are extended, so that it is possible to write the pages without taking them out of the binders. When the book is closed, the cords hold the papers tightly and there is little chance of tearing. Extra pages can be removed and inserted simply, without taking out all the others. Having decided on this system you will then need one *Lecfile* and several *Shelfolds*.

The Lecfile

This fancy name is meant to indicate that you take only one loose-leaf binding cover to all lectures. It is hard-backed, with cords, not rings, and contains a number of stiff card separators. Some are supplied with the cover and others can be made from scrap card later.

The Shelfolds

These are also binding covers with cords, of the same size as the Lecfile but of inferior quality. They need be only manilla, since they will rarely be taken out of your room. They will remain on your shelves; hence the invented name. When your notes are growing in volume they are much too valuable to be carried around and perhaps lost. Take as little as possible with you in the Lecfile and leave the Shelfolds in your room. If you intend to study in a library during the day take the appropriate Shelfold with you, but only one. More would be cumbersome and you are probably wise to restrict library study to one topic at a time.

How to Make Notes

Notes are made so that they can be readily available to help your studies. To make what are commonly known as 'voluminous notes' is a contradiction or at any rate an acknowledgement that you have not yet decided on why you are making notes. If they are voluminous, they are not notes — if they are notes they are not voluminous. From whatever source knowledge comes, the notes must be brief and must cover the essentials in a few words. You cannot afford to wade through pages of scribbles, finding that most of it is of no value. You make notes so that you can extract, at a glance, the basic information you seek.

There are at least five major sources from which information may be extracted and put into note form — *lectures, private reading* in textbooks and technical papers, *conversations, seminars,* and *experimental work.* All of these are sources of information, opinions and deduction relating to topics and sub-topics. It is clearly foolish to compile five different sets of notes to cover these five sources. Rather there should be only *one set* of notes for each subject regardless of source. Ideally, you should have a duplicate set in some different place from the first — we could tell you daunting stories of lost notes. However, the duplicate set is an unapproachable ideal unless you are reading for a higher degree, in which case it is sound policy. You must merely be very careful of your notes, which will eventually represent much investment of time and labour. Price that at trade-union rates and you will be so frightened as to consider insuring them! If you are to have one set of valuable notes, don't lend them even to friends!

Waste Paper

The word *waste* in this context is both an imperative command and an adjective. From the appearance of most students' notes one would assume that there is a continuing strike in the paper-making industry. Pages are written closely and amorphously from side to side and from top to bottom. If you do this you have lost a great deal of value in the notes. If you expect to receive information from several sources for a particular topic, the space allocated to that topic must be large, so that later notes can be added. Thus large blank areas must be left for further use. It is in this responsible way that we use the word 'waste' as an imperative command.

But you will say, 'Paper is too expensive'. Why? Because students will insist on using not simply new unused paper but paper that has been punched for them, wrapped in transparent plastic, and sold in small quantities at high prices. We have no wish to ruin the stationers who make a profit in this way but, if you are studying and making notes correctly, you will need vast quantities of paper, which you clearly cannot afford to buy in this costly fashion. You may well require a pile of paper about a foot high, because the techniques employed require wide margins and much blank space.

Now we come to 'waste' as an adjective. Collect used paper that is blank on the back. Backs of letters, circulars, committee papers and advertisements can all be used. Most of these are now in A4 size but, if they are not, they should be reduced to this size. If they are smaller, staple them together as a pad for rough calculations. Waste paper might be obtained from a friendly printer. Printers have to consign large quantities of clean paper to waste, and it does not matter what size they throw out; accept it if it is available. Ask all your friends in business to save sheets of A4 that are blank on the back. Persuade a couple of typists to do the same. If you have access to old drawings from an engineering firm, jump at the opportunity of getting them. They are probably in A1, A2 or A3 sizes. Simple folding will bring them down to A4. Old computer print-out is another possible source.

Having got the paper, whatever the colour or quality, you will need two

other tools. One is a *double punch* for perforating the sheets. Get a strong
one. The extra cost is worthwhile, for you can then perforate a bundle of
sheets at once. Make sure that the spacing of the holes suits your corded
Lecfile. The second tool is necessary only if your paper source is supplying
sizes bigger than A4. It is a *guillotine*. Drawing paper of the larger A sizes
should be folded appropriately and cut with the guillotine through the folds.
The resulting paper may be a millimetre or two smaller than A4, but this is
not critical. Warning: it is dangerous to let your mind wander when using the
guillotine. The backs of dyeline prints make very good writing surfaces. You
would not be reading this book now if we had had to rely on 'refills' for
student notebooks. We try to give the publisher new paper, but the drafts of
these chapters were all done on the backs of once-used sheets. Paper
circulates today in vast quantities, and you need only to retrieve some of this
to provide yourself with an adequate body of notes at no cost at all.

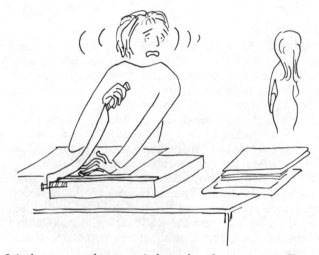

It is dangerous to let your mind wander when using a guillotine

   Assuming that you take this advice and collect used paper or cut some to
suit your purpose, what next? Your notes are not to be imperishable works of
art, but merely businesslike tools to help you in your studies and in reaching
the standard required by examiners. Set up a high pile of paper, blank on one
side. Square it up, and measure to the centre of one long side at various points
down the pile. Join these with a heavy line drawn by a marker or a felt pen;
the line must be thick and bold. You will find that each sheet then has a small
black mark in the centre of the long side, and this can be set against the
centralising mark that your punch must have (if it doesn't, don't buy it). In
this way, the papers will all be identically punched, and will lie neatly in the
Lecfile and Shelfolds. There is no need to spend time punching the whole pile
at once — take a few sheets when needed and punch them immediately
before use.

A Day's Note-making

Carry the Lecfile with you, containing perhaps two or three of the last sheets that you were working on at the previous lecture. You should have with you a page on which you have noted difficulties and doubts to be cleared up with the tutor. If there are several lectures or seminars that day, carry the appropriate note sheets for each course, separating the different notes with the card dividers. Blank pages with two broad margins drawn on them should be inserted for the day's notes.

Your notes are not imperishable works of art

The whole business of listening to lectures is discussed elsewhere (chapter 3) but it is worth emphasising here that note-making is not concerned with taking down every word that a lecturer says. Unless you are a very competent shorthand writer you cannot do this, although most students seem to try. The amount of notes you should take depends on the content of the lecture, your familiarity with the topic and the availability of the same material in textbooks and hand-outs. In our opinion you should aim for outline notes with the more difficult parts expanded in greater detail. In order to do this, however, you have to listen intelligently to the lecturer and think about what he is saying. Regretfully not all students do this. On one occasion a professor became aware when lecturing that not a single eye was raised from the all-consuming task of rapid squiggling. Without changing his tone of voice he broke into a tale of an elephant who entered the garden the night before and ate the cabbages. It was at least a quarter of a minute before anyone looked up, and there is little doubt that the word 'elephant' appeared on the pages of these so-called notes.

On arriving back in your room after a day at college, you should *immediately* (don't leave it until later) transfer the day's pages of notes to the individual Shelfolds that have been allocated one to each course or subject. The Lecfile should now, once more, contain only the tail-end of the notes to serve for continuity for tomorrow's classes. In the course of the evening or the next few days you may come across some new information or viewpoint relating to the lecture that you attended. If so, get out the appropriate Shelfold and add the relevant note. In this way you will soon build up a comprehensive set of notes for revision.

Each of your topics in the appropriate Shelfold should be recorded on consecutively numbered pages. It is essential to be strict about numbering. If you are not, the sheets will take a long time to re-assemble if they are accidentally dropped. In addition to the number at the top right-hand corner of each page (not in the middle or at the bottom), there should be some code of initials and numbers referring to the sub-topic in that particular Shelfold. This sounds complicated, but it isn't. For example, what you are reading now was typed on a page headed MN/3dr/10. This meant that the subject was Making Notes; that it was the third draft (for other drafts were lying about); and that it was the tenth manuscript page of that draft. The sheet was then unlikely to get out of place.

Making Attractive Pages with Punch

If you take down notes by writing from edge to edge of the paper, leaving no blank spaces and no outstanding features, you will make very heavy weather of re-reading the notes during regular study or in preparation for an imminent examination. For quick revision, the skeleton of the subject must be visible at a glance, and it is worth while making some effort to produce this effect, if only for ease of revision; indeed, revision becomes almost a pleasure if the notes are eminently readable and carry their message with punch. Each of your Shelfolds of notes compiled from lectures, seminars and private reading must be of such a form that the message leaps from its pages. Use some or all of the following ideas (and add your own) to bring punch to your notes.

(a) *Make liberal use of headings and sub-headings.* Break up the text as much as possible into topics, sub-topics and conclusions — or some such skeletal division of your own — using *key words* (which are discussed below).

(b) *Expand headings into the left-hand margin.* A glance down the left-hand margin then gives a quick summary of the work noted on that page.

(c) *Expand conclusions into the right-hand margin,* noting all the decisions reached in the study of the subject. A glance down the right-hand margin then shows what you have learnt.

(d) *Use coloured pencils* according to a code of your own devising, perhaps by underlining in colours representing the measure of importance of the key words. Colour is best added during study; during lectures you have no time to decide on relative importance, so do not underline anything in pen or pencil. Do it later in colour.

A mnemonic or memory-jogger is sometimes useful. Wide margins, the suggestions given above and colour coding during study periods make for an attractive and useful set of notes. Your mnemonic is CHIC, which is what your notes ought to be

C: Conclusions in the right-hand margin (40mm wide)
H: Headings in the left-hand margin (40mm wide)
I: Inside the margins for the notes
C: Colour for punch.

If your notes have CHIC they will be in an excellent form for fast and effective study and revision — one of the main reasons for making notes at all.

The Instant Final Shape

When you attend your first lecture — one of the occasions when every student considers note-making to be obligatory — you will, no doubt, feel conscientious. Most students feel this way for a week or two. Perhaps, with this sense of purpose still fresh upon you, you decide that the notes taken during lectures will be 'written up' in your room — when? Later. This would perhaps be a laudable idea if it were possible of accomplishment. But to make a trim and coherent job out of a mass of scribbles is, Dear Reader, nothing but a pipe dream. It has the result of making your notes illegible and unusable — for, after all, aren't they to be put into immaculate form later? Not likely! There are far too many pressures on your time: there will be no time left for 'writing up later'. In an undergraduate course there is never any time 'later'; there is only 'now'. 'Now' is better used in study than in unprofitable re-writing of what should have been done well in the first place.

In your professional work after you have qualified, you will rarely be allowed time to do everything twice and so you had better learn now. Whether you make notes at a lecture, in the library or from textbooks that you are reading, they must be the finished article in its final shape, except for the colour coding indicating ranges of importance. It is not easy to produce the instant final form of a body of notes, a single skeleton compiled from diverse sources. However, once the technique has been mastered, and provided lots of space is left, making a set of notes with powerful punch and instant accessibility gives as much sense of achievement as going round the golf course under par or making a successful rugby try against strong opposition. *Always write in a finished form.*

Contents of the Shelfolds

So far we have tried to impress on you the importance of having one set of notes rather than a mass of different notebooks or scraps of paper. We have suggested that your notes are too valuable to be carried about, but that with *one* Lecfile you can take down all that is required from various lecture courses and from reading in the library. We have warned against the use of too many words in your notes. They must be brief and include lots of spare blank paper to be filled up later. We have told you about making wide margins, which will give you a quick view both of the skeleton of the subject and of the important findings and memorable conclusions of the study. We have plugged the idea of colour for punch. But we have said nothing yet about what you are to put in the notes. Here are some ideas.

Every lecture course is divided into sections, usually listed in the published college syllabus. These sections will be broken down and explained by the lecturer, and further understood in your reading. But the student who goes to his first lecture without any idea at all of what he is to face is working quite inefficiently. You should start by trying to produce a skeleton of each of the sub-headings in the syllabus. Your lecturer will be delighted to find someone taking a positive and active interest in his subject, and will be willing to help — if you don't take up too much of his time.

The secret of success in this task is finding the *key words* that make up the skeleton. Key words have been much used in recent years in the retrieval of information. By taking the subject GEOGRAPHY, then a major division such as HUMAN, a third division URBAN and a fourth one NEW TOWNS, the body of the subject can be penetrated in detail. The technique is shown in the next section.

The Shelfolds containing the gold nuggets of opinion and information that you have dug up will be written round the key words. These should be determined before the study starts, as far as possible. This statement may seem nonsense, since you have no idea of how the lecturer is to tackle the subject, but by means of a pattern diagram you can build up a picture of what your studies are to contain. This can be shown by carrying out the few steps necessary, and so below you will find a worked example of key words and patterns.

Key Words

Your notes should consist chiefly of *key words* linked by blank spaces in the first instance. Later study will fill in the spaces with key words of lesser rank, until the whole topic is built up into a coherent and connected body of knowledge. Lecture notes should never consist of many words, for the presence of such a mass of words will make the notes difficult to assimilate and understand at a later stage. In the lecture periods use extreme simplicity in note-making.

First of all, take a part of a subject that you are studying and write down the key words that give the basis of that aspect of your studies. To find the key words, look up this basic topic in *several* textbooks in the library or from your own shelves. You will be surprised at how differently the authors look at even an elementary subject. By writing down their key words, taken from headings within the chapter, you can have in front of you parallel but different patterns of the same subject. But however different these patterns may be, key ideas will be repeated in each, and by the time you have written down the key words referring to your topic from half a dozen texts, you will be halfway to having the skeleton articulated. As an example, take the subject of bending moment and shear force, which any student of mechanics has to study.

We picked five textbooks at random, each textbook containing a chapter on shear force and bending moment. The differences in treatment of the authors was very apparent when we found that some selected a few headings and sub-headings and others sub-divided the subject much more. The numbers of key words that we picked out from the five authors were 7, 17, 7, 16 and 12. Putting these down in any order, we found, after removing duplicates, that we had 23 key words.

When you get to this stage, you should write the key words down as shown below. Do not try to form them into any sort of order; merely pick them out and write them down. You should use one word for each idea, if possible, but sometimes two are necessary.

MOMENT : DIAGRAMS : SHEAR : RELATIONSHIPS : LOADING: UNSYMMETRICAL : CURVED BEAM : 'STANDARD' CASES : THRUST : FUNICULAR : GRAPHICAL : INTEGRATION : INCLINED LOAD : VERTICAL LOAD : CONCENTRATED : DISTRIBUTED : INCLINED BEAM : NON-UNIFORM LOAD : SHIPS : SIGNS : SUPERPOSITION : POINTS OF INFLECTION : NUMERICAL SOLUTIONS : APPLIED COUPLES

The Pattern of Notes

If you knew what the lecturer controlling your studies was to do in the way of arranging these in a particular order, you could make a skeleton in linear form, one heading following another and falling into a hierarchy of importance. In the absence of this information, it is sound practice to make a secondary arrangement of key words; they cannot be left as they are above, for they make sense only as their interrelation is explicitly shown.

The pattern diagrams advocated by Tony Buzan (his book *Use Your Head* (B.B.C. Publications, 1974) is well worth reading) give an excellent diagrammatic arrangement; the main topic occupies an oval lozenge, around which the main sub-topics cluster, while the lesser branching of less important subjects extends further out. Figure 2 shows one way of displaying the interrelationships between the key topics, but there may be others. All the key words above are used except SHIPS (merely another example of distributed loading), UNSYMMETRICAL BENDING (not applicable in view of the conditions given in the central lozenge) and CURVED BEAMS (also irrelevant).

We feel quite sure that, if you have followed this technique carefully, you have a much clearer mental framework within which to carry out studies of bending moment and shear force than you had before. The same technique can be applied to any other topic, but always use as many textbooks as you can. One or two will not do — but then what's a library for? Work in the library and also use your textbooks.

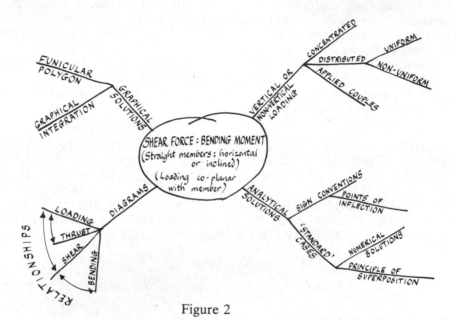

Figure 2

Notes of Notes

Whatever you do, and however you compress and simplify your notes, they will still occupy considerable space. But you have organised your knowledge, supplemented the printed expositions and stimulated your memory. The final step is to shorten your notes still further. They can be used to simplify the skeleton of the topic still more, until it stands out in its bare bones, giving you a framework on which memory can hang the developments, opinions and controversies. These notes of notes we are calling, in the vulgar tongue, *swot cards*; they are referred to more particularly in chapter 7. They form the ultimate distillation, but must not form the only aspect of your studies; the skeleton must be clothed, and study must be pursued into all the ramifications of the life's work to which your books and papers direct you. To that end, a body of notes over which you have 'sweated blood' is a pearl beyond price.

Think and Act

Think (A): Viewpoint

You should look on your notes as you would on a stamp collection — small, frequent additions on the right pages and plenty of empty space for more in the same category. For each subject, use one set of notes only, built up from many sources and giving facts, opinions, questions and controversies.

Think (B): Skeleton

The outline of your notes should be based on the syllabus or programme of the subjects and built up from *key words* abstracted from textbooks and other writings on the topics concerned. Make a pattern diagram (figure 2).

Act (C): Constant Presence

During lectures, keep the Lecfile close to you; during study, use the Shelfold of the topic. Never read or listen without being ready to enter a note in the appropriate place where space has been left for such a possibility. Notebooks must be a constant presence. Give them punch!

Act (D): Waste Paper

Develop a passion for collecting A4 paper that is clean on one side only. Get friends and relatives interested. You will need a great deal of paper if your notes are to be kept useful. Several pages of notes may become full; in that case, two pages must be inserted in place of one, allowing the notes when transferred, to be spread out and empty spaces restored. If you find that this expansion is really necessary for the same sub-topic on several occasions, you may be sure this is an important and perhaps developing aspect of the subject, and therefore one deserving more than normal attention.

Develop a passion for collecting A4 paper blank on one side

5
Using the Library

A significant proportion of what you are studying today will be out of date in the space of a few years. But don't be dismayed — this is unimportant provided that you have learnt during your studies how to find out for yourself, to think for yourself and to express yourself. This is what true education is about. The essence of it is summed up in the old proverb: 'Give a man a fish and he is satisfied for a day: teach him how to fish and he will be satisfied for the rest of his life.'

Unfortunately, too many students take what seems the easy way out, and try to remain tied to their tutor's apron strings throughout the course, relying on him for detailed notes and guidance. What a waste of ability and resources! Excellent as the tutor/student relationship may be, it has failed if the teacher, in satisfying your thirst for knowledge, has not taught you to depend on yourself. In the hard world of industry and commerce the tutor will not be there to give guidance — *you will be on your own.* Anyway, it is a short-sighted policy to rely too heavily on the tutor for detailed guidance since, good as he might be, he is unlikely to have a monopoly of knowledge in his particular subject.

In your own interests it pays to seek the opinion of other experts through their writings. There is a vast store of knowledge in the world on every conceivable subject and this has been painstakingly recorded in textbooks, journals and a variety of other publications. This collective knowledge and experience of many of the world's experts is available to you if you are prepared to find the appropriate publication and read it.

The knowledge now available in published form is bewildering and exciting: bewildering because of its sheer volume and complexity; exciting because most recorded knowledge is available to you individually at little or no direct cost. Just ponder for a moment on that staggering fact — *practically the whole store of recorded human knowledge in the world is available to you as an individual at little or no direct cost.*

By this stage of your career you will have built up a small personal library comprising books of great variety. These will probably range from ephemeral paperbacks to more substantial tomes purchased for your studies at college, as well as others probably given to you as presents on special occasions. The creation of a good personal library is a habit to be encouraged; now is an excellent time to begin, when you are purchasing books for your degree studies.

However, good and indispensable as personal libraries are, they are of necessity puny when compared with the whole store of human knowledge.

This knowledge is available in recorded form in books, journals, pamphlets, microfilms and microfiche in general and special libraries. Your own college library and local lending and reference libraries house a great deal of this; you will be able to borrow or refer to the literature in these libraries. However, it is clearly impossible for each library to hold all the publications that you could conceivably require. To overcome this difficulty, colleges and public libraries have grouped together to form inter-library loan schemes. If a particular publication is not available at your own library the librarian will almost certainly be able to obtain it on a short-term loan. In this way an individual reader has access to practically the whole of recorded knowledge. Remember that the library is the heart of a college: you should make it your second home. And find out details of inter-library loans.

You should make the library your second home

Classification Systems — Order from Chaos

Bearing in mind the difficulty that you may have had even in locating a book on the shelves in your room, imagine what a formidable task it is to arrange hundreds of thousands of books in a college library in such a way that each reader can quickly find a particular book or publication on a particular topic. This problem has exercised the minds of librarians throughout history. The basic principles of ordering or classifying books are straightforward and, as long as the number of volumes is small, little difficulty is experienced. But with the rapid increase in the number of books and documents published each year, and also in the range of topics covered by these publications, the complexity of classification has increased correspondingly.

During the last century six major classification schemes have evolved — Dewey Decimal, Brown Subject, Universal Decimal, Library of Congress,

Bliss' Bibliographic and Colon. Of these, by far the most popular and universally used is the Dewey Decimal Classification. Because most of our readers will be using libraries that have adopted this system, fuller details are given below, together with a brief description of the Universal Decimal Classification, which is based on the Dewey system. Should your library use some other system a full description will be available from the librarian or his staff. Do not hesitate to ask.

The Dewey Decimal Classification

Melvil Dewey, a famous librarian, devised the decimal classification system and published the first edition of it in 1876, when he was 21. History records that, after months of study, Dewey was thinking about the problem during a long sermon in church. The solution suddenly came to him, and he had to control himself from shouting out 'Eureka'. Since the first publication, the system has been revised at seven- or eight-year intervals and the eighteenth edition was published in 1971. It is certainly the most used general classification system in the world, and is probably the best for public and general libraries. It is universal in the sense that it is used on all five continents.

Dewey reasoned that the whole of human knowledge could be divided into the following ten broad classes

000	Generalities
100	Philosophy and related disciplines
200	Religion
300	The social sciences
400	Language
500	Pure sciences
600	Technology (Applied sciences)
700	The arts
800	Literature (Belles-lettres)
900	General geography and history

Each of these classes is then divided into nine divisions, and these in turn can be divided into nine sub-divisions or sections; zero is reserved for books of a general nature. For example, a book numbered 510 is in class 5 Pure sciences, division 1 Mathematics and is of a general nature, that is, the book is on mathematics in general and not limited to any one section. On the other hand, a book on algebra would have the classification 512 meaning class 5 Pure sciences, division 1 Mathematics, section 2 Algebra. Thus every book and pamphlet in a library using the Dewey classification has a particular class number giving class, division and section. Books are arranged on the shelves in a simple decimal order.

Among the beauties of the Dewey Decimal system are its simplicity and the universal appeal of its notation, which can be easily understood and applied. Moreover, Dewey gave an undertaking that no drastic changes would ever be made in the allocation of numbers to subjects, although certain modifications have been made in recent editions. The accepted divisions and an example of how a particular division is split into sections are given below. These show that every publication has a class number consisting of *at least three digits*, but the system permits further sub-divisions allowing as fine a division as is thought to be necessary. For example

624	Civil engineering
624.1	Structural engineering
624.15	Foundation engineering
624.151	Foundation soils and engineering geology

The 100 Divisions

000 Generalities
010	Bibliographics & catalogs
020	Library & information sciences
030	General encyclopedic works
040	
050	General serial publications
060	General organizations & museology
070	Journalism, publishing, newspapers
080	General collections
090	Manuscripts & book rarities

100 Philosophy & related disciplines
110	Metaphysics
120	Knowledge, cause, purpose, man
130	Popular & parapsychology, occultism
140	Specific philosophical viewpoints
150	Psychology
160	Logic
170	Ethics (Moral philosophy)
180	Ancient, medieval, Oriental
190	Modern Western philosophy

200 Religion
210	Natural religion
220	Bible
230	Christian doctrinal theology
240	Christian moral & devotional
250	Local church & religious orders
260	Social & ecclesiastical theology
270	History & geography of church
280	Christian denominations & sects
290	Other religions & comparative

300 The social sciences
310	Statistics
320	Political science
330	Economics
340	Law
350	Public administration
360	Social pathology & services
370	Education
380	Commerce
390	Customs & folklore

400 Language
410	Linguistics
420	English & Anglo-Saxon languages
430	Germanic languages German
440	Romance languages French
450	Italian, Romanian. Rhaeto-Romanic
460	Spanish & Portugese languages
470	Italic languages Latin
480	Hellenic Classical Greek
490	Other languages

500 Pure sciences
510	Mathematics
520	Astronomy & allied sciences
530	Physics
540	Chemistry & allied sciences
550	Sciences of earth & other worlds
560	Paleontology
570	Life sciences
580	Botanical sciences
590	Zoological sciences

600 Technology (Applied sciences)
510	Medical sciences
620	Engineering & allied operations
630	Agriculture & related
640	Domestic arts & sciences
650	Managerial services
660	Chemical & related technologies
670	Manufactures
680	Miscellaneous manufactures
690	Buildings

700 The arts
710	Civic & landscape art
720	Architecture
730	Plastic arts Sculpture
740	Drawing, decorative & minor arts
750	Painting & paintings
760	Graphic arts Prints
770	Photography & photographs
780	Music
790	Recreational & performing arts

800   Literature (Belles-lettres)

810   American literature in English
820   English & Anglo-Saxon literatures
830   Literatures of Germanic languages
840   Literatures of Romance languages
850   Italian, Romanian, Rhaeto-Romanic
860   Spanish & Portugese literatures
870   Italic languages literatures   Latin
880   Hellenic languages literatures
890   Literatures of other languages

900   General geography & history

910   General geography   Travel
920   General biography & genealogy
930   General history of ancient world
940   General history of Europe
950   General history of Asia
960   General history of Africa
970   General history of North America
980   General history of South America
990   General history of other areas

Technology (Applied sciences)

600   Technology (Applied sciences)
601   Philosophy & theory
602   Miscellany
603   Dictionaries & encyclopedias
604   General technologies
605   Serial publications
606   Organizations
607   Study & teaching
608   Collections & patents
609   Historical & geographical treatment

610   Medical sciences
611   Human anatomy, cytology, tissues
612   Human physiology
613   General & personal hygiene
614   Public health
615   Pharmacology & therapeutics
616   Diseases
617   Surgery & related topics
618   Other branches of medicine
619   Experimental medicine

620   Engineering & allied operations
621   Applied physics
622   Mining engineering & related
623   Military & nautical engineering
624   Civil engineering
625   Railroads, roads, highways
626
627   Hydraulic engineering
628   Sanitary & municipal engineering
629   Other branches of engineering

630   Agriculture & related
631   General techniques & apparatus
632   Plant injuries, diseases, pests
633   Field crops
634   Orchards, fruits, forestry
635   Garden crops   Vegetables
636   Animal husbandry
637   Dairy & related technologies
638   Insect culture
639   Nondomestic animals & plants

640   Domestic arts & sciences
641   Food & drink
642   Food & meal service
643   The home & its equipment
644   Household utilities
645   Household furnishings
646   Sewing, clothing, personal grooming
647   Public households
648   Household sanitation
649   Child rearing & home nursing

650   Managerial services
651   Office services
652   Written communication processes
653   Shorthand
654
655
656
657   Accounting
658   General management
659   Advertising & public relations

660   Chemical & related technologies
661   Industrial chemicals
662   Explosives, fuels, related products
663   Beverage technology
664   Food technology
665   Industrial oils, fats, waxes, gases
666   Ceramic & allied technologies
667   Cleaning, color & related
668   Other organic products
669   Metallurgy

670   Manufacturers
671   Metal manufacturers
672   Ferrous metals manufactures
673   Nonferrous metals manufactures
674   Lumber, cork, wood technologies
675   Leather & fur technologies
676   Pulp & paper technology
677   Textiles
678   Elastomers & their products
679   Other products of specific materials

680	Miscellaneous manufactures	690	Buildings
681	Precision instruments & related	691	Building materials
682	Small forge work	692	Auxiliary construction practices
683	Hardware	693	Construction in specific materials
684	Furnishings & home workshops	694	Wood construction Carpentry
685	Leather & fur goods & related	695	Roofing & auxiliary structures
686	Printing & related activities	696	Utilities
687	Clothing	697	Heating, ventilating, air conditioning
688	Other final products	698	Detail finishing
689		699	

The promise given by Dewey not to alter the subject numbers obviously has clear advantages but at the same time has built-in disadvantages. For example, the growth in knowledge across the subject divisions originally put forward by Dewey has been far from uniform, with the result that some of the classes are desperately overcrowded, while others are relatively empty. However, the Dewey system, which allows for infinite sub-division on a decimal basis, can cope with this. It does mean that for certain growth areas in technological subjects the class number is very long, For example, the subject 'Short Take Off and Landing Aircraft in the United States' has the class number 629.1333404260973. Note that the decimal point appears only once, after the first three digits.

Many subjects are represented in a standard form or treated in a standard way and, to cater for this, each edition of the Dewey system lists standard sub-divisions that are never used alone but may be *added* to any number from the general subject tables. For example

- -01   Philosophy and theory
- -02   Miscellany
- -03   Dictionaries, encyclopaedias, concordances
- -04   General special
- -05   Periodicals
- -06   Organisation
- -07   Study and teaching
- -08   Collections
- -09   Historical and geographical treatment

A book dealing with the historical and geographical treatment of foundation soils and engineering geology would require an extension to the number given above; it would become 624.15109. These standard sub-divisions are, of course, given in much greater detail in the official classification tables. For example, a few of the sub-divisions of -07 are

- -071   Schools and courses
- -0711   Colleges and universities
- -0712   Secondary schools
- -0715   Agencies for adult education
- -07154 Correspondence courses
- -072   Research
- -0724   Experimental

Thus a publication dealing with experimental research in foundation engineering would be classified 624.150724 if the librarian felt that such a fine
classification was necessary.

In addition, the official classification index includes an area table, which
lists common geographical divisions. For example

-4   Europe
-5   Asia
-6   Africa
-7   North America

Each of these is sub-divided, an example being

-4   Europe
-41   Scotland and Ireland
-411   Northern Scotland
-4111   Shetland Islands

The use of these area-table numbers can be illustrated in the following two
examples

624.15109411   Foundation soils and engineering geology in
               Northern Scotland (note the use of 09 before the
               area notation)
508.6   Scientific surveys in Africa (since no confusion
               can arise in this case, 09 is not necessary).

These are given for illustration only, since in practice the first would almost
certainly be classified under 624.151 along with all the other books on
foundation soils and engineering geology.

The underlying principle of the Dewey Decimal Classification is extremely
simple and any complexity arises from the inter-disciplinary nature of books.
However, the reader need not worry about this, since the task of classifying
rests with trained librarians. Provided the reader knows the system in
operation in the library in which he is working, he can trace all the
publications he requires through an intelligent use of the catalogues.

Universal Decimal Classification

This system of classification was initiated by the International Institute of
Bibliography, which was formed towards the end of the nineteenth century.
The Institute, now re-named the International Federation of Documentation,
set out to design a standard international classification scheme primarily for
documentation rather than for general library use. The Universal Decimal
Classification is based on the main sub-divisions of the Dewey system with
certain modifications. In addition, the three-digit minimum of the Dewey
system has been contracted to eliminate unnecessary zeros, and the decimal
point appears after every three digits to break up the number. However, the

strength of the Universal system lies in the auxiliary tables, which are a development of the Dewey standard sub-divisions and area tables. These are supported by a series of symbols used to indicate relationships between subjects and standard sub-divisions through classes. A full description is beyond the scope of this work but the following will serve as examples.

Colon :. This is the main innovation and is used where a subject has to be represented by two concepts from the classification. For example, Sociology of Law would be entered as 34:301 (that is, 34 for Law and 301 for Sociology).

Brackets ( ). If the first digit within the brackets is a zero this indicates the form of the publication; for example 54(03) means Chemistry (dictionary of); 82(091) means English Literature (history of). If the first digit in the brackets is other than zero then a physiographic or geographic location is indicated; for example, 591(285) means animals (pond); 385(410) means Railways (in Britain).

Equals within brackets (=). An equals sign within brackets is used to indicate race when a geographical number is not sufficiently precise; for example, 94(=924) is History (of the Jewish People).

At first sight these symbols look very formidable, but with a little practice they can be mastered and understood. However, it is important to realise that they are used only if the main table numbers do not adequately classify the document. The Universal Decimal Classification was devised with a very fine specification, and as such is found to be useful for technical libraries and for information retrieval. At the moment, therefore, its use is mainly limited to technical libraries and enjoys nowhere near the support of the Dewey Decimal Classification system.

Catalogues — The Keys to a Library

Undoubtedly, the keys to the publications in a library are the catalogues, which are housed in a prominent position for easy access by the readers. They usually consist of banks of card-index drawers. Used intelligently, they enable the reader to trace any of the books or documents in the library.

Name or Author Catalogue

The name catalogue is usually, but not always, on cards filed alphabetically under the author, editor, institution or body responsible for the work. Where the work is best known by its title, it is filed under that title. A typical card gives details of the author(s) or editor, the title of the book, its edition, publisher and date of publication, total pages, illustrations, etc., subject-class mark and size, that is, octavo (small), quarto (larger), folio (very large) or the equivalent in centimetres or inches.

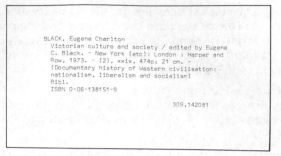

```
BLACK, Eugene Charlton
  Victorian culture and society / edited by Eugene
  C. Black. - New York (etc): London : Harper and
  Row, 1973. - (2), xxix, 474p; 21 cm. -
  (Documentary history of Western civilisation:
  nationalism, liberalism and socialism)
  Bibl.
  ISBN 0-06-138151-9

                                309.142081
```

Specimen Printed Card

This represents the maximum of information that normally would be found on a card, the minimum being the author, title and subject-class mark. The following special procedures apply.

(a) *Joint Authorship.* There is a card filed under each author's name up to a maximum of three.

(b) *Editors.* The card is filed alphabetically under the name of the editor.

(c) *Names of Societies, Institutions, Government Departments or Other Bodies.* For works published under their auspices the card is filed alphabetically under the name of the society or institution.

(d) *Names of Conferences.* Conferences are entered under the title of the conference. Proceedings of the conference issued or sponsored by societies or institutions usually have an additional entry under the name of the society or institution. Also, there is normally an additional entry under the editor.

(e) *Anonymous Works.* These are entered under their titles, for example, *Encyclopaedia Britannica.*

Subject Index

This index, often on cards, gives in alphabetical order the subjects together with their class numbers.

```
SOCIAL  CONDITIONS        309.1
```

Specimen Printed Card

Subject or Classified Catalogue

Usually, subject-catalogue cards are filed numerically by the classification number of the subject of the book. This catalogue is used to check the books that the library holds on a particular subject.

309.142081

1973

BLACK, Eugene Charlton
Victorian culture and society / edited by Eugene
C. Black. - New York [etc.] : London : Harper
and Row, 1973. - [2], xxix, 474p ; 21 cm. -
[Documentary history of Western civilisation:
nationalism, liberalism and socialism]
Bibl.
ISBN 0-06-138151-9

Specimen Printed Card

Periodical Catalogue

Periodicals (or serials as they are sometimes known) are listed alphabetically by the title as it appears on the title page of the periodical. Some periodical catalogues have a subject arrangement. The complete holdings of each periodical title are listed on one or more cards. Where the entry ends with the words 'to date' or a dash, this means that the library holds a complete file of that title from the date given.

JOURNAL OF LINGUISTICS
v.1 1965 to date

Index
V.1 lacks index

Specimen Printed Card

Other Catalogues

Many libraries have separate catalogues of special material that is excluded from the name, subject and periodical catalogues. For example, separate catalogues are often provided for manuscripts, maps, projects, reports, theses, translations and Government publications. Find out how *your* library is arranged.

How to Find a Publication

What you know about classification systems and the catalogues is now sufficient to be put into practice. Remember: 'practice makes perfect'.

Let us assume that you want to find a particular book and that you know the title and author. As you enter the library, you will see the catalogues in a prominent place. You should look for the author's name in the name or author catalogue. You will possibly find a number of cards under his name, each detailing one book under his authorship. Find the card giving the title of the book that you seek. If you cannot find the card, it could be for one of two reasons: that the library does not hold a copy of the book; or that the book is of a special kind and is listed under one of the special catalogues. Assuming that there is a card, note the classification number and the symbol indicating the type of book, for example, q — quarto, f — folio, p — pamphlet. Most libraries have wall charts guiding you to the shelf groupings for the major Dewey divisions. When you find the area of the library in which the class number of your book is located, do not immediately look for it, but try to locate the range of shelving where the class number can be found on the spines of the books. Then, and only then, may you look for the individual volume. The larger books (folio) are often grouped together on the lower shelves of a particular stack or in a separate sequence of shelves. Also, for convenience, pamphlets are often grouped together in boxes or lateral files. If you cannot find the book on the length of shelf containing books of the same class number, then it is probably out on loan. There might be a faint possibility that it is being bound, although this applies more to periodicals than to textbooks.

It sometimes happens that you want to find a particular book but you have forgotten, or never knew, the name of the author. Then you should first look up the subject in the subject index. Having found the appropriate class number from the card, look for it in the subject or classified catalogue and flick through the cards of that particular number. If the book that you require is in the library there will be a card in the catalogue for it. Much the same procedure is followed if you are interested in a topic rather than in a particular volume. You will find the appropriate class number in the subject index. Find the shelves containing that class number and you will have access to all the books on that topic that are not out on loan. This technique gives you a broad view of the subject but the best books are probably in the hands of other readers. Make an intelligent use of the catalogues. Browsing, although pleasant, is inefficient. If a book is out on loan you will miss it completely. Also, if larger-than-normal books are stacked separately, or if special books are kept in separate collections, every book on the same subject will not necessarily be in the same place in the library. Also, an important book may be missed since it may deal with several topics but it can be shelved only in one position in the library. The subject or classified catalogue covers this by listing the book several times under each subject heading. Use the card index. If you wish to consult a periodical, find the periodical index, and remember that periodicals and special collections are usually housed separately from the books available for loan.

For Reference Only

Most libraries have a special room or section housing reference books, bibliographies, abstracts and valuable collections. These books are for reference only and are not to be removed from the library. Like any other book, however, they are listed in the catalogue, where they usually bear some distinctive mark such as R indicating that they are not available on loan.

Because certain textbooks are in great demand, colleges often set aside a student reading room in which are placed multiple copies of textbooks that have been recommended by the lecturers. Do not let this kindness on the part of the college discourage you from buying your own textbooks and building up a library of your own.

Libraries vary in design but many have a special room or area in which the current issues of periodicals are placed. Usually the bound copies of back numbers are housed on the stacks. We recommend that you visit the periodicals area each week, to keep up to date with one or two topics that particularly interest you.

The number of books, theses and bound copies of periodicals is increasing so greatly that many libraries have a serious storage problem. Because of this, some of the more bulky material has been transferred to microfilm (35 mm or 16 mm) or microfiche (6 in. × 4 in. or 5 in. × 3 in. transparencies). As an illustration of the saving in space, one microfiche can contain a whole journal of 100 pages. Special equipment is provided in the library to enlarge the films for reading.

Guides in Literature Searches

The current rate of increase in the number of books, periodicals and learned journals being published is exponential and it is very difficult for a student to keep abreast of developments in a particular field. For example, the number of books *currently* in print in the United Kingdom and North America is 650,000, in addition to the millions published since the invention of printing. During your undergraduate studies you should have little difficulty in tracing the information that you need, since most will be contained in well-known textbooks. However, in the preparation of final-year seminar papers and dissertations, or if you continue on at college as a research student, you will need to find out details of all the work that others have already carried out in the field in which you are interested. Fortunately there are a number of valuable publications to help you in your search, and listed below are brief details of a few of the more important ones. For a more comprehensive list refer to books such as *Guide to Reference Material* by A. J. Walford, *Guide to the Literature of Engineering, Mathematics and the Physical Sciences* by S. Goldman and *How to Find Out about the Social Sciences* by G. A. Burrington.

British Museum General Catalogue of Printed Books

This lists all the 5 million books in the library, in alphabetical order by author. The subject index is available for the period 1881 – 1960.

National Union Catalog

When completed this will list some 10 million books, which are housed in the Library of Congress and other major libraries in the United States. Taken together with the British Museum General Catalogue, a very significant proportion of all the books ever published is listed.

Cumulative Book Index

This index is claimed to be a world list of books in the English language. It is published monthly (except August) with annual and other cumulations and lists books by author, title and subject in a single alphabetical index.

British National Bibliography

This is a very full classified catalogue of British books published since 1950 with author, title and subject index. It is published weekly with monthly and other cumulations.

Books in English

First published in 1970, this index is issued bi-monthly with an annual cumulation, and lists the authors and titles of all books from American and British sources. The index is on microfiche.

Abstracts

The abstracting and indexing journals provide from articles published in periodicals and learned journals a valuable way of finding relevant information. However, they are now appearing in such large numbers that many libraries have prepared *Key word in context* (KWIC) lists, which give the range of subjects covered in the various abstracting and indexing sources available in the library.

Engineering Index

This is issued monthly with annual cumulations and is the most comprehensive work in the field of engineering. Articles and selected books are abstracted and arranged in alphabetical order of subject. The index is very well cross-referenced, which means that it can open up valuable new fields of research.

Science Citation Index

The S.C.I. indexes every article and every significant editorial item from every issue of over 2700 of the world's most important journals in over 100 disciplines. It is available from January 1961 and is published at three-monthly intervals with annual cumulations. The work consists of three separate but related indexes; Citation Index, Source Index and Permuterm Subject Index. The *Source Index* is an author index to all the articles published in the given time period. It provides full title, names of authors, journal name, volume, page number and year of publication. The *Citation Index* lists all the previously published items cited in the articles listed in the Source Index. The great value of this is that the searcher can look up the name of an author known to have published in the field of interest and, if any previously published work of the author has been cited, the item will appear along with the names of the citing authors. Thus a whole field of search will be opened up. In the *Permuterm Subject Index* every significant word from the title of every article covered in the Source Index is paired with every other significant word in the title. These pairs are alphabetically listed and linked to the name of any author who used them in the title of the article that he wrote.

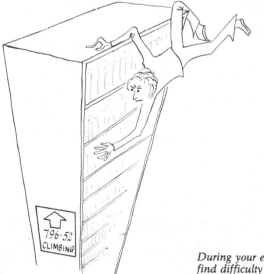

During your early days you may find difficulty in locating a book

If in Difficulties

Although the principles of classification and storage are straightforward, the mechanics and techniques can be complicated by the sheer volume of material to be dealt with. For this reason, particularly during your early days at college, you may find difficulty in locating a book. *If in doubt, do not hesitate to ask the library staff*. These people have been trained in librarianship, which is an art in itself. Moreover, they have been trained to serve and you will find them most helpful. The fact that they are helpful, however, is no excuse for your not becoming proficient yourself in carrying out library searches. All the tools that you need are there and with intelligent use you should be able to manage on your own most of the time.

The library staff have been trained to serve you

Think and Act

Think (A): Viewpoint

A library is where you go not to look for books but to consult an index or catalogue.

Think (B): Reference

You can leave a library without a book, but with information obtained from the Reference Section, from which books may not be withdrawn but only consulted. You can also keep up to date with your own subject in the Periodicals Reading Room.

Act (C): Book-finding

Track down the following books through the index. Are they in the library's catalogue? Are they on the shelf where they should be? Put in a request for one of them that is missing from the shelf, and see how the system works.

    (a)   *The Mill on the Floss* by George Eliot
    (b)   *The Meditations of Marcus Aurelius Antoninus*
    (c)   *The Golden Bough* by J. G. Frazer
    (d)   *Principles of Physical Geology* by Arthur Holmes
    (e)   *The Ascent of Man* by J. Bronowski

You must not look for the book until you reach the shelf carrying its class number. What is the earliest date of publication for each of these? (Consult cards, not the books.)

Act (D): Fact-finding

Go to the Reference Section of the library and, by using the books, answer the following quiz.

    (a)   What is the meaning of the word THRAWN? (Dialect dictionary)
    (b)   What are the hobbies of the Prime Minister or or your favourite Professor? *(Who's Who)*
    (c)   On what chart does the rhumb line appear as a straight line? (Encyclopaedias)
    (d)   What are the dates of birth and death of Lord Nelson? *(Dictionary of National Biography)*

Pull out and look through the books on either side of the four you have had to use. You will now have at least a nodding acquaintance with twelve reference books. If you are sensible, you will return and try again.

6
Writing Reports

You hurriedly get out of your car and go round to the rear. The other driver behind is already inspecting the result of the accident. 'You've bashed my car', you say, surveying the damage. 'It's going to cost the earth to put it right. I consider you are no gentleman.' Your language may, in reality, be somewhat more forceful than can be printed here but, however you phrase it, you have in effect made a report. You have: (a) stated a fact; (b) drawn a factual conclusion; and (c) expressed an opinion.

These three parts — *facts, conclusions, opinions* — form the skeleton of a report. Reports may be brief or lengthy but they follow the same pattern. The problem to be studied is defined, and the facts known about it are listed. From these facts conclusions are drawn. But the 'technical' report — *and this includes not only scientific reports but those on any topic that requires study and elucidation* — cannot stop there. At the end there must be recommendations or opinions — an expression of what the writer considers has happened, will happen, or should happen. These opinions are based on the factual conclusions, but also must depend heavily on the experience of the writer of the report and on his knowledge of the subject under consideration.

You are not likely to be asked to write a report on a complex or recondite subject at the stage that you have reached in your studies. You will be dealing with simpler problems. Most college courses require you to write essays, laboratory reports or dissertations. These should all show the pattern

    (a)   collect facts
    (b)   decide what these facts reveal
    (c)   make a statement of your opinions.

Often students are either nervous of venturing into the third field or ignorant that opinions and recommendations are required to complete the report. They frequently write laboratory reports that give all the facts about an experiment or test but then come to an abrupt halt. Tutors are then tempted to write in large letters: 'SO WHAT?' If the problem is to determine and report on the suitability of a particular kind of steel for the construction of a bridge, an elaborate description of the tests carried out and the results obtained is not a full technical report, however excellently written. The question asked was: 'Is *this* steel appropriate for safe use in the building of *this* bridge?' Unless an answer is given to the question, the report is useless. The answer is reached through the factual conclusions on tests and from the experience and knowledge of the writer. He should know much about steel and about bridges and be capable of combining this knowledge with the undoubted facts revealed by the tests. The third part of the report — the opinions and recommendations — is the crucial section. Always be willing to make recommendations definite and positive; they should need little 'hedging' or qualification. The reader must be in no doubt as to what you think should be done about the problem. It is not enough to give him the facts.

The reports studied in this chapter are 'technical'; that is, they are not written in general terms but refer to a specific problem within a specific set of conditions. They necessarily have a narrow compass. They may be written in a college course or in the practice of a profession. They may be 'internal reports', which are those passing between parts of the organisation employing the writer. They may be 'external' or 'public', when they go outside the parent organisation. Whatever aspect they present — whether written for scientific or commerical purposes, or perhaps for some voluntary organisation — they will follow the lines of this chapter if they are to be of use.

Examples of technical reports might be

> A college report on a short experiment in mechanics
> A thesis for a higher degree in anthropology
> The findings of a young worker during Voluntary Service Overseas, on the social conditions in an African village
> The conclusions and opinions reached by the holder of a travelling scholarship on the variations in educational opportunities in several countries
> Findings on the depopulation of the countryside of S.W. England in the last 100 years
> Financial recommendations on a proposed merger of two large companies
> Economic proposals on the purchase and distribution of sugar in the E.E.C. countries.

In order to teach by example, the techniques of writing reports have been presented in the rest of this chapter by compiling a *Report on Writing Reports*. The shape and size of this report is representative of the middle-sized report. Some of its sections and their sub-divisions may be found unnecessary when applied to a particular problem; some may require to be expanded. What is given in the following pages may be regarded as a skeleton, to be clothed so as to suit the conditions of a particular report.

Whatever the type or destination of a report, and whether its length is several pages or several volumes, it should start with a registration of the following information

> (1)   the origin of the report
> (2)   the destination of the report
> (3)   the subject of the report or its terms of reference
> (4)   the date of the report
> (5)   a summary of its findings.

With these points in mind, turn now to the *Title page* and the *Introductory presentation* and note how these are expanded by techniques presented in the *Sections* of the report, leading to the *Conclusions* and the *Recommendations*.

MESSRS REPORT - WRITERS LTD

SALFORD, GREATER MANCHESTER

REPORT ON THE PREPARATION,

WRITING AND PRESENTATION

OF TECHNICAL REPORTS

BY

CASSIE W.F. AND CONSTANTINE T.

REPORT NO. CCC/CC/6   JANUARY   19····

Summary

Technical Reports are divided into three main parts — *the prelims, the body, the addenda*. The *prelims* comprise the title page, the contents, any list of mathematical or other symbols required and the summary. The *body* contains, under headings and sub-headings, the main arguments of the report, with final conclusions and recommendations. The *addenda* comprise — where appropriate — appendices, diagrams and tables, descriptions of equipment and method, acknowledgements and sometimes a technical abstract and a preface (which is added just after the title page). The terms of reference must be defined in advance, and appear in writing in the opening statement. The chief attribute of all reports should be brief, clear and precise English. Reports are always subjected to much criticism and it is only by writing in unexceptionable language for a specific readership that clear meanings are preserved. The author should imagine at his elbow a Querying Counsel criticising and cross-examining every phrase and sentence and pouncing on every lapse into 'jungle' English or common jargon. All the detailed notes, comments and drafts used in the preparation of the main report should be retained for reference in a second private report. For practice in the art of report writing, it is recommended that the suggested ideas are used where appropriate in the preparation of lab. reports, seminar papers and even private correspondence. Whatever is good in the writings of others should be copied, and constant reference should be made to such books as an English grammar, *Roget's Thesaurus* and a good dictionary.

Terms of Reference

This report was commissioned by Mr and Ms Reader, of Argyle College, University of Barchester, BARCHESTER. The terms of reference were the following.

> The authors are required to isolate, identify and categorise the problems facing the writers of reports. They are asked to produce a specimen report, listing those features that they consider to be important. Particular attention is to be paid to the use of English in the structure of the report. The findings should assist Mr and Ms Reader to become familiar with the craft and to be able to recognise and practise the techniques required in the preparation of a report.

CONTENTS

1.0 THE PRELIMS

In the publishing world, the *prelims* are the pages that precede the main text. In the pattern diagram of appendix 1, the prelims normally used in a report are displayed on the left of the diagram. They may not all be required in every report you write, but you must be familiar with their functions.

1.1 The Title Page

The title page shows a minimum of four items of information: *number, title, address, date*. In addition, the *author* of the report may be mentioned.

1.1.1 The Number of the Report

It is very important that a particular report can be found quickly, even after years; it might be needed to establish some point or to provide evidence in an argument or court case. It must, therefore, have a number linked with whatever filing system is in use. This number must appear on the cover and on the title page. So that the searcher can go directly to whatever shelf or filing case is appropriate, the number may have to be complex. Complexity is no disadvantage, so long as the report can be produced and the dust shaken off in a few minutes.

1.1.2 The Title

The title should adequately describe the report. There should be no attempt to shorten it to newspaper-headline form. Sometimes covers for reports are made with rectangular 'windows' that display the title on the title page, even when the report is closed. If this technique is used, the title must be carefully located on the title page so that it — together with the filing number and date — is visible in the window.

1.1.3 The Address

This is the address of the individual or organisation preparing the report.

1.1.4 The Date

The date must always appear on the title page, where the month and year are usually sufficient. Also the exact date of signing the report should appear at the end, under the signatures of those who accept responsibility for the report's findings.

1.1.5 The Authorship

Sometimes the names of the authors of the report appear on the title page but, if the report is going out in the name of an organisation, it may be kept impersonal except for the signatures at the end. These appear at the end of the body of the report and before the appendices and other addenda.

1.2 The Summary

You must take great care in writing the summary, which usually appears immediately after the title page or as part of the opening statement. The summary should give a brief statement of the contents of the report, but in writing it you should give particular attention to the conclusions and recommmendations. The summary is for the reader who is in a hurry and wishes to know quickly what the recommendations are. The rest he leaves to others.

1.3 The List of Contents

If the report runs to more than a few pages, there should always be a list of the various sections and headings to be found in the report. The contents list not only directs the reader to the page where he can obtain specific information, but also gives a quick survey of the structure and form of the report. When a large number of tables and figures appear in the report, the contents page is often extended to incorporate a list of the tables and figures. When a report is long it is sometimes split into two volumes, one with factual findings and a second whose contents deal entirely with discussions and recommendations.

1.4 The List of Symbols

Symbols are useful, not only in mathematical work, but also in obviating the necessity for repeated explanations. One symbol — perhaps merely a letter of the alphabet — can indicate a complex quantity or idea. Symbols are useful on charts, for example. The reader should be able to find the meaning of the symbol quickly. The custom of describing symbols in the body of the text, at the stage when the symbols are used, is to be deprecated as not being sufficiently accessible. If symbols are used the reader should be able to study a code list, which should appear immediately after the contents page.

2.0 THE BODY

The body of the report starts with an opening statement There then follow sections and sub-sections discussing in detail the facets of the problem for which the report was written. These sections form the major part of the whole publication and require the greatest attention from you, the author. Factual conclusions are then made, using the data and findings put forward in the textual discussion. This ends the reporting of facts and of supporting evidence.

The final sections give the report your personal stamp. They contain your interpretation of the factual conclusions, and go on to recommend what steps should now be made towards solving the problem that you were given. The report ends with your dated signature (and with others if more than one author is involved).

2.1 The Opening Statement

The statement should follow immediately and smoothly after the title. It should describe who commissioned the report and, if necessary, why it was required. The statement should also contain the terms of reference, and the summary should appear somewhere in these opening paragraphs.

2.1.1 Who Is to Read the Report?

A novel is written for the person 'in the street'. A report is aimed at a particular reader who is expecting and may have asked for facts, conclusions and recommendations. The report is, therefore, directed at amuch smaller target than the novel. There can be no scatter.

You may think that you know who is to read your report. You may have been instructed by a superior in your organisation to solve a problem by writing a report on it. But do not assume that he will be the only reader. There may be others after your superior has seen it. Find out before you start what your first, second and subsequent readerships will be. Is it to go to all the members of your organisation, is it to be read by the Board of Directors only, is it to be studied by the upper echelon of the scientific staff, or is it for the eyes of your boss only?

This information is essential to the successful writing of a report, so ask for it. Many a report has been unsuccessful, not because it was badly written, but because the writer visualised one type of reader, whereas, in the end, the report ended up in front of someone entirely different. If the Technical Director reads a report he can be informed by means of technical phrases and arguments. However, the Chairman of Directors would probably be lost with such a treatment, but would understand an 'everyday' layman's interpretation of the problem. Be sure of your readership and keep them in mind when writing. Be aware of the level of their expertise; adapt your statements to suit the background of the reader.

2.2 The Terms of Reference

A report should be a very precise piece of writing. It is produced solely to answer a defined question or to solve a defined problem. Before you start on the preparation you must be quite sure of the range of studies within which you are to work. Anything outside this range has no place in the report. If the terms of reference you have in mind are not precise, or if they are not explicitly stated, you may not go far enough in your investigations or you may stray outside the limits that your boss or client has in mind.

Suppose you are told: 'Jimmie, let me have a report on that fractured pipe'. You study the circumstances of the accident and its results; you investigate the strength of the metal and the pressures developed. Your report is precise and accurate and you put it on the boss's desk. He thumbs through it, glances at the summary and goes red in the face. 'Here, Jimmie, come here. I asked you to tell me who was to blame! You haven't said a ******* word about that! Who are you trying to protect, eh?' You got the terms of reference wrong because they were badly stated; so everything went wrong, and you got the blame.

It is best to get the terms of reference in writing but, if that is not possible, write out your version of the terms of reference. Send them to your boss's secretary, stating in writing that you are starting on the preparation of the report, as instructed, and are basing it on the enclosed terms of reference. Both you and the boss are now aware of what is happening. If he does not like the terms that you have submitted he will let you know!

2.3 Textual Discussion

The textual discussion on the subject of a report will be submitted to much more critical examination than any piece of creative or imaginative writing would be. A report carries no pages of poetry: fantasy is banished. It is an exercise in meticulous and exact communication. Here, more than in any other writing, every word must carry an exact and unequivocal meaning. Every unnecessary word, phrase or paragraph must be cut out. Your report must have an incisive bite, and bear directly on the terms of reference. Here is an example of a style that is too common.

> . . . Of course an operation like this has an extensive back-up requirement. There is an on-going situation in which the feedback is of maximum importance in assessing the viability of the project. We must operate to tight time scale and we must maintain a low profile throughout. Let those providing the service achieve a meaningful motivation from the enthusiasm in depth that they can see being generated for it. Price mechanism can be structured from cost-effective analysis to enable us to set a reasonable charge that will ensure profitability . . .

There are many ways of translating this; try for yourself. For example, the meaning might be expressed as follows.

> . . . This plan requires more staff. Over a period, public support will show whether the result is justified. We have little time. We must keep quiet about what we are doing. We hope that those serving will

be encouraged by the satisfaction that they give. We can adjust our charges to obtain a worthwhile profit . . .

It is often assumed that textual discussion must be complex to be acceptable. This is not true, for the purpose of a report is to communicate precise ideas and recommendations; this is best done in unequivocal terms into which only one meaning may be read. Brevity assists this aim.

2.3.1. Brevity

Brevity, so far as it is consistent with intelligibility, will be your over-riding aim in report writing. Those who ask for reports have no time to read long ones, nor will they take the trouble to unravel texts like the example given above. Readers of reports like brevity: they first read summaries; they leave the heavy matter and the appendices to juniors. Thus, if you want your report read by someone who has the authority to implement your proposals, be brief and incisive.

A year as a sub-editor on a newspaper would be an excellent apprenticeship to the disciplines required in writing a report. You would become accustomed to looking for the ambiguous and the turgid, to cutting the text down to its basic message. The reluctance of the amateur to abandon any of his precious passages is illustrated in an old jingle. It must have been written by some exasperated editor receiving streams of verbose articles from amateur authors.

> If you've got a thought that's happy
> Cut it down!
> Make it short and crisp and snappy;
> Cut it down!
> When you feel 'twould be a sin to
> Cut another sentence into,
> Send it in and we'll BEGIN TO
> Cut it down!

It urges you to examine every sentence, to tighten the sense. Every word must carry weight. It also reminds you that if you don't cut it expertly to obtain this effect, the professionals will, and you may not like it. Remember that you are a professional when you write a report. Don't indulge in the verbosity of the amateur, or try to hang on to an inappropriate bit of writing just because *you* wrote it.

2.4 The Querying Counsel

You can impress on yourself the need for clarity of expression, meticulous accuracy and brevity by imagining, while writing a report, that you will have to defend the completed version in court under cross-examination by an opposing Counsel. Think of yourself as an expert witness while you are writing your report, even if it is only a lab. report. The term 'expert' does not mean that you are very clever; don't get that idea! It indicates that this witness, unlike ordinary witnesses in court, is not held solely to facts. He is allowed, and even expected, to give opinions. Remember that your evidence as an expert witness must be based on the factual truth expressed in your report. If clarity and precision is not your ever-present aim in writing every report, an opposing Counsel will find you easy prey in his cross-examination. Therefore, whatever communication you present in writing, always imagine a *Querying Counsel* at your elbow. Write so that he cannot twist your meaning so as to make you agree to opinions the opposite of those you hold. He can be a deadly enemy; keep him there in imagination. He will help your writing.

2.4.1 The Report Eviscerated

To eviscerate, in this context, is to 'deprive of vital content' and this is exactly what opposing Counsel is in duty bound to do. He wishes to show that your evidence is not of the value that you think it is. Imagine that someone has been killed in an industrial accident. He has been caught in a machine, or some part of a machine has suddenly broken, with fatal results. The insurance company brings an action to try to establish that your firm showed negligence and was at fault. You are called as an expert witness on behalf of your firm, because you wrote a report on this machine and its maintenance and repair. The report was filed five years previously; the opposing Counsel has a copy and, you may be sure, is thoroughly familiar with every page of it. If you were wise at the time, you will have had a second report bound up and filed, containing every fact used, every reference studied, all the results of tests, every reason you had in mind when you drew your conclusions — and you alone will have access to these private notes. The format of this second report is discussed in the next section. You must also study what you said, so long ago, in the published report. With a court action pending, you may well be horrified to find what loopholes you left to the attack of a cross-examining Counsel.

At the hearing, your own Counsel takes you through the report and shows what a splendid, reliable fellow you are, and gives you questions that bring out the excellence of everything you did. When opposing Counsel rises to cross-examine you he seems just as genial, but beware!

Assume that your report contained a sentence such as the following.

> 'In the majority of cases the metal concerned had sufficient strength to resist the considerable forces deployed from time to time.'

The Querying Counsel might cross-examine you as follows.

COUNSEL: Now if you will refer to page 61 of your excellent report, you will see that you say that considerable forces were deployed.
YOU: Yes, that is so.
COUNSEL: Can you tell the Court, please, the magnitude of these considerable forces?

YOU: That is not a simple matter; we know that they were very large.

COUNSEL: Very large; perhaps twenty-thousand kilonewtons?

YOU: Perhaps that is somewhat on the high side.

COUNSEL: Well, shall we say 500?

YOU: No, that would be too small.

COUNSEL: Then the range is somewhere between 20 000 and 500 kilonewtons?

YOU (getting a bit lost): Yes, I suppose so.

COUNSEL: Don't you think, Mr Technol, that this range really means that you cannot put a figure to these considerable forces?

YOU: It is impossible to be precise under the conditions that we encountered.

COUNSEL: So you don't really know whether the forces were large or very large; your term 'considerable' has little real meaning in regard to this case?

YOU: I suppose that's true.

COUNSEL: Turning now to another part of the same statement, although you do not know the magnitude of the forces, perhaps you can tell the Court what you meant when you used the words 'from time to time'? How frequently were these unknown forces found to be acting?

And so it goes on. Bit by bit, he shows that you don't know the value of the forces nor the frequency with which they appeared. You flounder over 'the majority of cases'. You waver over 'sufficient strength'. In the end the opposing Counsel has apparently shown that you don't know what you are talking about. He will probably get you to agree the opposite of what you thought you said, as he did with 'considerable'. Of course, this is quite unfair, and the case probably does not even rest on that passage in your report. It was merely a passage (sufficiently relevant to be acceptable to the judge as a subject of cross-examination) that could be used to raise doubts in the minds of those in Court as to your ability to pronounce on the matter under trial.

This aspect of the writing of reports has been exaggerated to impress on you that *every* report, even the least important, must be able to stand up to expert cross-examination. Remember, all the time you are writing, the sport that a *Querying Counsel* could have with your uncertain presentation. In the example invented, you would have been on much safer ground if you had written a precise account, as follows.

> 'We took 50 routine measurements of stress on each of 25 occasions between 25 February and 17 June. On 65 per cent of these occasions the mean stress developed was 82.7 per cent of the BS requirement for safe loading. The maximum stress during the period was 97 per cent of the BS safe stress.'

This would be much more difficult to discredit, especially as you would have with you extracts from the second report giving standard deviations and other statistical facts for these tests. These would be kept in reserve by you until they were required in answer to cross-examination. Always read the report you are writing like a learned barrister determined to open up ruthlessly even the smallest crack.

2.5 The Second Report

Brevity, as we have deliberately repeated, is important in the published report. Clear and unequivocal English is a necessity if the sense of your report is to be incontrovertible. But this does not apply to the 'second' report — the one that is not published but kept in your files. This second report is your armoury against questions and attack in the future. There may never be a court action — such an experience is uncommon for the average report writer — but criticism and attack you will certainly encounter. If you make sure that you have the ammunition to beat the fictitious Querying Counsel, you can fend off the attacks of your own organisation.

The second report is a carefully written and elaborate record of everything that you did and thought during the preparation of the report. The dates on which these sections and thoughts took place are also carefully recorded. Dates often assume more importance than you would imagine to be possible.

If you carried out experiments with plant or equipment the detailed readings you took must be retained in their original and dated form. For this detailed recording of facts, opinions and deductions the hard-bound students' notebook is better than the loose-leaf systems recommended in chapter 4. In a bound book there is less chance of anything being lost — especially if you write in ink so that there can be no later alterations. In the bound notebook and accompanying drawings, reference and photocopies of data, there will be the factual answer to any query. Drafts that you made of the report and later improved or discarded should also be retained. All this mass of material must be written so that others may understand it. No private abbreviations or squiggles should be permitted. Neither should you omit something because it is so familiar to you that is seems silly to write it down. When the file comes to be consulted you may be in another part of the world, in hospital or long dead! There is a story that when the Ordnance Surveyors started to revise the original primary triangulation of the United Kingdom, they looked up the notebooks of more than a century previously. They found one entry referring to some specific survey station that read: 'See Mrs Jones at the farm; she knows where it is.' This may be an apocryphal story but illustrates the importance of ensuring that your notes will be meaningful to others, even long after they are written.

2.6 Making Yourself Understood in English

The following ten sections select a few of the aspects of the technique of using your native language effectively. They represent by no means all that could be said: only study and practice can lead you to develop the ability to produce clear and precise meanings through the written word. Try to develop a feeling for the pleasures of language. Winston Churchill, when he was a young officer in India, read for four or five hours a day, developing his knowledge and love of English. In *My Early Life* he says

> I had picked up a wide vocabulary and a liking
> for the feel of words fitting and falling
> into their places like pennies in the slot.

All through his life he used words with power: the active voice; the short sentence; few adjectives; few qualifications of principal clauses; his books are models of what writing in a technical report should be.

2.6.1 Basic Rules of Good Writing

Accepted authorities on the writing of good English prose — the Fowler brothers and Arthur Quiller-Couch — agree on three rules that make for effective writing:

(1)   Prefer the familiar word to the far-fetched.
(2)   Prefer the concrete expression to the abstract.
(3)   Prefer the single word to the circumlocution.

These were the first three of five rules pronounced by the Fowler brothers, and with these three Quiller-Couch agrees. The fourth and fifth were as follows.

(4)   Prefer the short word to the long.
(5)   Prefer the Saxon word to the Romance.

Quiller-Couch is a little doubtful about these two. For simple statements they certainly apply, but O. says that, when you begin to philosophise about the 'why' and the 'how', the Romance words are required. In spite of this slight difference of opinion, accept the first three rules as fundamental to good writing, with the other two in use most of the time.

The other habit you should develop is to use the *active voice* rather than the *passive voice*. In the active voice the subject of the verb is the doer of the action. This construction leads to strong and direct writing.

'We wrote this report'

is in the active voice. The passive voice is much weaker in the impression it makes. Then the object of the action is turned round to be the subject of the verb

'This report was written by us'

It seems to be accepted that impartiality and an impersonal flavour to the report are achieved by the use of the passive voice. (This sentence is in the passive voice because the words 'impartiality' and 'impersonal' were the ones we wished to fix in your mind as you read the sentence.) But there is no reason why you should write a report in an impersonal manner. If it is written by one person there can be no objection to an occasional 'I', and if by several persons to the use of an occasional 'we'. Cultivate the active voice to avoid weakness in your writing.

2.6.2 Know Your Words

Like Churchill, try to develop a wide vocabulary. One of the best ways of achieving this is to buy a copy of *Roget's Thesaurus of English Words and Phrases*. There are paperback versions, but we advise you to buy a hard-backed volume, for it will have much use. It has been well-used in writing this book. You may have come across *Roget* as it is affectionately called, but we are willing to bet that not many of our readers habitually use the book or have it on their shelves. *Roget* gives, in one paragraph, words and phrases that are closely related to a word or a phrase that came into your mind but is not quite right for the sense you are trying to convey.

Suppose you have in mind the word 'jargon'. In our copy of *Roget* it is listed as follows

> Jargon
>   absurdity, 497
>   no meaning, 517
>   unintelligible, 519
>   neology, 563

You can be quite sure that if you examine all these numbered sections you will find every word in the English language that is remotely or closely equivalent to 'jargon'. Nouns, adjectives, adverbs and verbs are all given. As an example, if we look at the nouns only, we have

> in section 497: more than 50 nouns, such as farce, burlesque, twaddle, mummery, *jargon*, moonshine, mare's nest, etc.

> in section 517: more than 50 nouns, such as nonsense, *jargon*, gibberish, jabber, hocus pocus, rant, bombast, palaver, verbiage, platitude, etc.

> in section 519: about 30 nouns, such as unintelligibility, obscurity, ambiguity, paradox, enigma, riddle, steganography, asses bridge, *jargon*, etc.

> in section 563: nearly 40 nouns, such as neology, caconym, archaism, lexicon, missaying, antiphrasis, thesaurus, *jargon*, concordance, lexicology, etc.

Thus, if you want to describe words which are *absurd, with no meaning, unintelligible, new or used in a new sense*, you have the choice of about 170 nouns — including 'jargon', the one you first thought of — available for your selection and use. In addition to these nouns there are verbs, adverbs and adjectives in similar numbers. No one writing a report should be without a *Roget's Thesaurus*.

2.6.3 Know Your Prepositions

One of the features of modern technical writing has been the gradual elimination of the preposition. This is the result of competition in the newspaper world to produce as much information or pseudo-information in a headline as is verbally possible. The method is to use a string of nouns — usually short nouns, so as to save space. Two or three nouns in succession are used as pseudo-adjectives qualifying one of their number. Although this may be acceptable for newspaper headlines, it must be avoided in technical writing. The temptation to use the 'substantival–adjectival' technique is great and is far too common in technical writing. Resist it: use your prepositions.

The chief objection to the use of several nouns as adjectives is that the sense is very much obscured. For example

> Bomb incident probe demand

This is clearly a newspaper headline and can be excused. It means that there has been a demand <u>for</u> an investigation <u>into</u> an incident <u>with</u> a bomb. The prepositions are underlined. But although newspaper headlines must be concise and use short words (an investigation is always a 'probe' and an ambassador is an 'envoy') there is no excuse in technical writing. Here are a few examples from published technical papers. If you don't understand them, you don't surprise us, but they were not invented

> compliance calibration curve
> fracture toughness measurement
> measurement science material
> crossing route choice study
> steel strain distribution curve
> end shear span
> glassware supply situation
> standard crack width formula

Sometimes this compression produces an amusing result

> Council probes flat flood

The sense has gone completely here. One has a vision of the Council members poking sticks into flood water! Surely they know already that a flood is flat! What is meant — but not said — is that the Council has investigated the cause of a flood in a tenant's flat. Or

> Art rings enquiry ruling

No, Arthur is not pulling on a bell rope! The meaning is that a ruling has been made <u>on</u> an enquiry <u>into</u> 'rings' developing <u>in</u> the art world.

You will often be tempted to use this kind of gibberish. The examples are too frequent; they must have an unsuspected influence on readers of newspapers or technical papers. The antidote is to know how to use prepositions. When the noun–adjective comes in, the use of the preposition decays, with loss of intelligibility. We need precise and concise statements but sense must not be sacrificed to the aim of reducing the number of words.

Just to remind you, here are a few English prepositions

> by, down, for, in, of, off, on, over,
> under, up, with, without.

See if you can fill in some more. Look up a good book on grammar and work on your prepositions.

2.6.4 *Know Your Punctuation*

If you look through this book you will find we have used the semi-colon and, less frequently, the colon. These punctuation marks are not sufficiently used in technical writing and can be of assistance in preparing reports.

The *colon* indicates the strongest possible break within a sentence and can be interpreted as meaning 'as follows'. It often comes before a list. For example, this book contains a number of chapters: Studying, Passing Examinations, Speaking in Public and others.

The *semi-colon* is used to link two clauses that are closely related and would sound disjointed if kept separate as two sentences. 'The student did not seem to know how to use the library; he was mooning about the shelves instead of consulting the index.' These two clauses could have been separated at 'library' but the semi-colon indicates that they are linked and that the second explains the first.

Neither of the above points of punctuation is sufficiently used, but the *comma* is probably over-used. It is often inserted where a semi-colon is needed to separate two independent clauses. For example; 'The author wrote many textbooks, he also wrote science fiction.' This punctuation is incorrect but regrettably is very common. Do not fall into this error. The correct punctuation in the example is as follows: 'The author wrote many textbooks; he also wrote science fiction.'

The comma is unusual before 'and' and 'or' but can be used when 'and' separates two ideas. 'The student was carrying his books and his pocket calculator.' There is no need for punctuation within that sentence. 'Henry was carrying his books, and suddenly he saw Sheila in the distance.' A comma has been used here to separate the two distinct impressions, but some might think it unnecessary even there. A comma is certainly correct in that last sentence before 'but' because there is a change in direction of thought.

2.6.5 *Know Your Paragraphs*

We must assume that you know how to express yourself in sentences. The totality of English grammar is too great to be studied in detail here; there are numerous books on the subject. However, the question of the proper construction of paragraphs deserves the attention of any report writer.

It is not enough to change to a new paragraph at intervals just because you know that a block of text is always broken up in this way. There are three attributes that you should look out for and try to develop in your paragraphs. The *first* is that the paragraph should develop a specific part of the topic being considered. Only when that topic is fully discussed can you sit back and think 'what next?' and move on to the next paragraph. The *second* attribute is that each paragraph should have as a first sentence a brief statement or at least an indication of what the paragraph is to consider. The first sentence in this paragraph, for example, indicates that the discussion is to be about the change from one paragraph to another. The *third* attribute is that the final sentence in a paragraph should, ideally, form a link and a lead-in to what is to be discussed in the next paragraph. If there is nothing more to be discussed, then a new heading appears in the report and you move on to another subject.

2.6.6 Jungle English and the Fog Index

Jungle English was the title given by A. P. Herbert to writing so confused that one has to read each sentence several times, struggling with the words to find some sense like someone caught in a jungle. One longs for a machete to cut a way through. Many translations have been made from direct to jungle English as warnings to writers of reports. Probably the most famous is A. P. Herbert's own translation of Nelson's famous signal

> England expects that every man will do his duty.

The irreverent but salutory translation reads

> It is anticipated that, as regards the current emergency, personnel will face up to the issues involved and exercise appropriately the functions allocated to their respective age groups.

Haven't you seen that kind of thing recently? Are you guilty of jungle English? It is fatally easy to fall into the habit. English is such a rich language and has gathered so much from many linguistic sources that you must consciously choose and reject words if you are to write well. Selection and rejection are guides to clearer writing.

A splendid example of translation into jungle English was published by C. Porter in *The Liverpool Post*. The original version was Hood's *Song of the Shirt*

> Work, work, work
> My labour never flags.
> And what are its wages?
> A bed of straw,
> A crust of bread and rags!

Porter's translation uses the well-known phraseology and verbosity of official pronouncements

> Maximised productivity, maximised productivity, maximised productivity. My industrial activation is never subject to unco-ordinated recessionary tendencies. And what is the prescribed extent of the statutory diurnal remuneration? A nocturnal sleeping unit of unprocessed cereal material, an exterior segment of medium calorie farinaceous comestible and attrited fragmentary clothing units.

Well that may be a bit of fun, but it is quite possible for you to write in a complicated manner without realising it. You should keep a close watch on yourself, to make sure that you do not stray from the clear and concise presentation of your facts and opinions. To assist you in this, a quick check on how well your writing can be understood is provided by the *Fog Index*. This measure of comprehensibility was devised by Robert Gunning. The following procedure will give you a rating of the readability of your writings.

(1) Select a number of consecutive sentences whose combined wordage is not much under or not much over 100.

(2) Divide the number of words by the number of sentences to give an average measure of words per sentence.

(3) In the same text, marking off exactly 100 words, count the number that have three or more syllables. This gives the percentage of 'longe' words in the text. You may omit from this count words that begin with a capital letter, words that are long because they are hyphenated and verbs whose third syllable is '-ed' or '-es.'

(4) Add the count from (2) to the count from (3) and take 40 per cent of the total. This number is the Fog Index. The higher the index the less comprehensible is the text.

Admittedly, this is a somewhat crude measure of readability, but an excellent guide in your efforts to produce a good technical report. It is obvious that a philosophical discussion may well have a high Fog Index and yet be comprehensible to the initiated. Higher values of F.I. can be expected for material that requires study, but for reports your aim must be to make the meaning clear on the first reading.

The figure to keep in mind is 12. Below this value the F.I. indicates that the text is comprehensible; above 12 the F.I. indicates that you had better shorten your sentences or use less elaborate words or both. Here are two extreme examples at opposite ends of the range to let you assess how close your writing is to one or the other. Simple subjects, treated simply, have a low F.I. This example is typical. We wrote it for you.

> The cat sat on the mat. Nursie was sitting too, but not on the hearthrug. She was knitting and singing a song. The kettle on the stove sang to itself and the sun was sinking in the west. A warm, golden light shone through the window. In the garden the roses were blooming on the bushes. They were pink and white beacons in the twilight. Peter, the pony, stood silent in the field. Was he thinking about the oats he would have in the morning? Nursie got up and drew the curtains. The room was lit only by the firelight.

In this passage the Fox Index is about 3. Now consider the following example. We also wrote it expecially for this chapter. It does have a meaning (we think), but you are in the depths of the rain forest!

> The machine-based fundament of modern civilisation has emanci-pated even those most exposed to severance from the requirements of life; broader and less mutilated existence become a viable

possibility. The widespread distribution of opportunities for tertiary education occurring during the preceding decades has extended its development into broader opportunities for communal leisure activities. Let us expurgate from the immaturity of our environmental thought, that essence of crepuscular darkness which our sciolism leads us to extrapolate into quotidian existence. Occupational background can emblazon the personality with unmistakable illumination for the endeavours we make towards a better and more acceptable society.

In this case the Fog Index is about 23, double the maximum for easy reading.

Check your Fog Index at intervals. Don't let the fog gather. If the F.I. rises substantially above 12, have an inquest and shorten words and sentences.

2.6.7 In Defence of Proper Jargon

What A. P. Herbert called jungle English is often called 'jargon'. This word has two principal meanings. One is *confused unintelligible language* and the other *the technical terminology or characteristic idiom of a special activity or group*. We have dealt with jargon in the sense of confused unintelligible language. Now let us have a look at proper jargon as it applies to technical reports.

Between knowledgeable writers and readers, the use of proper jargon, which is technical and precise, is perfectly acceptable. But remember that the language and vocabulary may be incomprehensible to the readership of your report. You must, therefore, be prepared to translate the jargon of your profession into normal, crisp English if your readership requires it. In dealing with a financial problem to a readership composed of professional economists or bankers, it would be correct to include in your report passages such as the following:

> In retrospect, the buoyancy of equities relative to fixed-interest securities seems less a reflection of any positive preference or near-inflationary consideration than a mere short-term re-adjustment of the converse position.

If you were to be talking in a discussion group on television, or writing an article for a widely read magazine, such a statement would then be quite unacceptable.

Do not be afraid of using your own jargon — the words and phrases dealing with your expertise — provided you are reporting to people in your own profession. If your report is to another audience, adjust your language to suit them. This is very difficult when you are accustomed to your precise and meaningful jargon, but it is a skill you must acquire if you are to be a successful communicator.

Do not confuse jargon of the technical kind with jungle English. Proper jargon uses a shorthand of technical words and phrases to simplify, for the knowledgeable reader, matter too complicated for everyday English. Jungle

English on the other hand, represents a deliberate change, within everyday writing, from direct to complex and less intelligible language.

2.6.8 Cloudy Phrases

'Cloudy' phrases are those that obscure the precise meaning of a sentence. They do not form as dense a fog as measured by the Fog Index, but when you use cloudy phrases a mist gathers. They can have no foothold in precise writing, such as the text of a report. However, such phrases do have their uses in speech. They are much used, for example, to buy time to think. The human brain works at the speed of a computer or faster, but some milliseconds are needed for thought. In answer to a difficult question before the television cameras you might say 'Well, really it seems to me, at this moment in time, that in connection with. . .' By that time your sub-conscious mind has drafted the real answer to the question.

But you are concerned with precise and meaningful writing where the more relaxed habits of impromptu speech cannot be allowed to creep in. Cloudy phrases must be eliminated. Listen for them on radio and television and look for them in the newspaper. Make a list of them and, when you write, avoid them. Most can be replaced by one or two words or by re-phrasing the sentence. At the same time look for the mixed metaphor, which occurs far too often and adds nothing (except humour) to the sentence. This one is taken from a recent letter to *The Times* newspaper.

> 'They have a first class officer who has leant over backwards to establish a low profile in dealing with immigrants.'

The emergence of new phrases is continuous; this is an attribute of a vigorous and developing language. Many original phrases, coined by keen minds for a specific occasion, have made strong impressions because of their freshness and force. Speakers of less originality, and writers too, pick up these phrases at second hand and use them until their first fire and punch are worn away. How many have tried to blow Harold Macmillan's *winds of change* when the context did not merit the phrase? How many have taken the edge off the phrase *at the grass roots* by applying it to inappropriate circumstances? How many people have been invited to *stand up and be counted* long after this phrase was first used?

Riots in the United States were once described as continuing through *a long hot summer*. This was a telling phrase, giving a feeling of oppression and dismay. But it has been used far outside its original setting. The phrase reached its nadir when a British politician threatened *a long hot legislative summer*! The reaction to this could only be ridicule. In the air-conditioned House of Commons, set in the English climate, and with the long recess allowing members to look for long hot beaches, such a plagiarism illustrated how not to employ catch-phrases of the day.

But it is not against original over-used phrases that we wish to give you the severest warning. The really insidious and mischievous phrases are the well-established ones that come to mind unbidden because we have heard them so often. They are like friends and are familiar and comfortable to the tongue, but are deadly enemies to clear and original writing. Let's look at a few of these confusing clouds and their real meanings.

2.6.9 Simple words and the Cloudy Phrases Often Used

The following list is by no means exhaustive.

Able	in a position to	False	not in accordance with the facts
About	with reference to		
Abundant	in considerable quantities	Fewer	a decreased number of
Admittedly	it is true that	If	according as to whether
After	subsequent to		
Agree	come to the same conclusion	Large	of considerable size
		Largely	in large measure
Allows	provides a means by which	Lasting	of considerable duration
Although	in spite of the fact that	Later	at some future time
		Less	a decreased amount of
Always	in all cases; in all instances	Mainly	for the most part
Apparently	it would appear that	Many	a considerable number of; a large number of
Because	owing to the fact that; for the very simple reason that; in view of the fact that		
		May	has a tendency to
		More	an increased amount of
Before	prior to; on a previous occasion	Most	the majority of
Betray	sell down the river	Much	a large proportion of; a considerable amount of
Can	is capable of		
Cannot	is unable to; is not in a position to	Near	in the neighbourhood of; in close proximity to
Commoner	encountered more frequently		
Conclude	come to the conclusion that	Now	at this moment in time; at the present time
Describe	give an account of	Often	in many instances; in many cases; on numerous occasions
Disagreement	conflict of opinion		
Enough	an adequate amount of; sufficient number of; in sufficient quantity		
		Previously	at an earlier date
		Rapidly	at a rapid rate
Enter	gain entrance to	Rare	of infrequent occurrence
Everywhere	across the board		

Rarely	in few instances; in few cases	Studying	engaged in a study of
Recommence	back to square one	Support	to be in favour of
Seldom	in a few instances; in a few cases	Think	incline to the view
		To	with a view to
Some	a certain amount of; a number of; a degree of	Virtually	to all intents and purposes
		Visibly	in front of your very eyes
Sometimes	on occasion; in some instances; in some cases	When	at the time when
		Where	in the place where
		While	during the time that
Somewhat	to some extent	With	in conjuction with
Start	from the word 'go'		

2.6.10 *Cloud Eliminated by Re-phrasing*

We do not say that the phrases listed above should *never* be used. Sometimes they have their uses in making the sentence flow more pleasantly or in avoiding too much repetition of the same work. However, there are some cloudy phrases that have little or no value. Some of them appear in the above list, for a hard line cannot be drawn. The phrases in this second category can be completely eliminated by re-phrasing the sentence and so improving its construction and sense. Here are a few examples.

> In connection with rose-growing, pruning should be in the spring.
> You should prune your roses in the spring.

> The snow will be of a heavy character (or nature).
> There will be heavy snow.
> ('Character' and 'nature' are often misused in this way: look out.)

> From the studying-communication point of view, I find this book useful.
> This book is useful when I study communications.

> With regard to what you owe me, I intend to cancel the debt.
> I intend to cancel your debt to me.

> There is a high degree of certainty that my friend will win.
> My friend will probably win.

> We have no intention to emigrate so far as present plans are concerned.
> We have no immediate intention to emigrate.

Try to become 'allergic' to such phrases as

In connection with	Relative to
If and when	On the basis of
From the point of view that	With regard (respect) to

Eliminate these and similar phrases from your writing and you will find its clarity and readability much improved.

A word that causes much obscurity, and is quite unnecessary in precise writing, is 'case'. Read Quiller-Couch on this word; he has a bit of fun with it. Note how it can be completely eliminated; the sentences can also be shorter.

> In every case the job was well done.
> All the jobs were well done.

> It was found in all cases that the fires had been accidental.
> All the fires were found to have been accidental.

> In this case it was fortunate he did not break his neck.
> He was fortunate not to have broken his neck.

> Deflections in the case of the other beam were small.
> In the other beam, deflections were small.

We have already pilloried jungle English. You will find that it too can be eliminated by re-phrasing.

> Positive consumer response is escalating.
> People are buying more.

> Intensive industrialisation is inevitable in a consumerised society.
> If we consume goods we must have many factories.

> Oil is dominated by deficiencies in the world-supply situation.
> The world's supply of oil is deficient.

May we, at this stage, say that a positive integrated progression is evident at this moment in time. In other words: NOW YOU ARE GETTING SOMEWHERE!

2.7 Conclusions and Recommendations

The *Conclusions* are those deductions drawn from the textual discussion. They refer to what has been studied and are factual. The *Recommendations* look to the future and describe what the author of the report thinks should be done about the problem that has been the subject of so much investigation.

2.7.1. Conclusions

The Conclusions should be presented as numbered points, as follows.

(1) Technical reports are divided into three main parts – prelims, body and addenda. The main textual discussion and final conclusions and recommendations come in the body of the report.

(2) The readership of the report must be known if the writing is to be in a style to suit the recipients. Technical jargon, in the

terminology of the profession concerned, may be used only if the readership consists of members of that profession.

(3) The terms of reference must be defined in advance to ensure that the author and his boss or client are agreed on what is being studied and what the final report should cover. These terms of reference should be in writing and should also appear in the opening statement of the report.

(4) The English of the report must be concise and clear; it is important to avoid cloudy phrases, in which the real meaning may be obscured. The active voice should be used wherever possible.

(5) The detailed notes, comments and drafts used in the preparation of the report should all be retained, put in order and filed. Both the report and this second report must be retrievable at a moment's notice even after years.

(6) Both conclusions and recommendations should be given in numbered lists. The addenda should be kept to as few items as are necessary for the proper presentation of the work.

(7) The whole report must be written in such clear and precise language that it is able to withstand cross-examination by Counsel.

2.7.2 Recommendations

The Recommendations, like the Conclusions, should be clearly enumerated.

(1) Model any reports you write at college on the layout given in this report. Some of the requirements may be unecessary but we urge you to adopt the suggested techniques wherever possible to give you the practice that is needed before you can become a competent report writer.

(2) Study the method of building the body of the report. The textual discussion will take a form dictated by the subject of the study. You should, however, absorb the recommendations of sections 2.1 – 2.5, which ensure that your report will be well based.

(3) Study section 2.6 and put the ideas into practice in all your writing whether it be a seminar paper, a lab. report or simply a letter home. At all times imagine the Querying Counsel looking over your shoulder. Where time permits, leave the final draft of any report you have written for a few days and then read it again with fresh eyes. Be honest and ruthless in your criticism.

(4) Read widely and be critical of the style adopted by other authors. Copy what is good; reject what is poor.

(5) Obtain several good reference books including an English grammar, *Roget's Thesaurus* and a good dictionary. Have them by your side while writing and *use them.*

Signed
W. F. Cassie ....

T. Constantine ....

11 January 19—

3.0 THE ADDENDA

The addenda consist of supporting evidence for the ideas put forward in the body of the report. In this report the only addenda are two appendices. In addition, there may be diagrams and tables, descriptions of equipment and procedures, an abstract, a preface, the index, and acknowledgements of assistance received during the preparation of the report. Many of these will be missing in some reports, and in others all or nearly all will be used.

3.1 The Abstract

This is rather more than the summary that appears in the prelims. If an abstract is included, it may be on a separate loose sheet and can be used to give in some detail the contents and argument of the report to those who do not require to read the whole text. It is by no means common to find an abstract but, when it does appear, it is often on an index card of standard size, which can be filed.

3.2 The Preface

This, again, is unusual. It is used only if the origin of the report must be described in greater detail than is possible in the opening statement of the body. It outlines the problems and may also include the reasons for presenting the report in the form given. It can include the acknowledgements, if these are not numerous.

3.3 The Index

An index would be prepared for a very large report but is somewhat unusual for the majority of reports. However, an index is *essential* for any volume containing many items to which reference is made by the reader. The index must be full and complete with plenty of cross-references.

Appendix 1

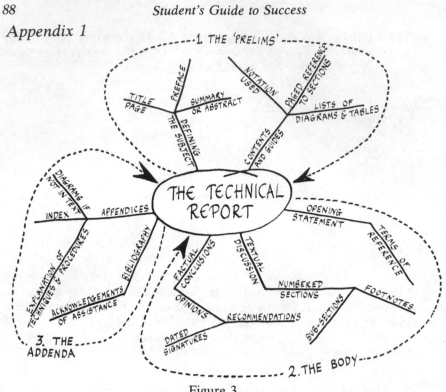

Figure 3

Appendix 2

It is very important that a Report can be found quickly, even after many years

The Chairman of Directors would probably be lost with a technical treatment

Every unnecessary word must be cut out

Don't try to hang on to an inappropriate bit of writing just because YOU wrote it

'Council probes flat flood'

Check your Fog Index at intervals

'They have a first-class officer who has leant over backwards to
establish a low profile in dealing with immigrants'

7
Passing Examinations

'History' said Henry Ford, 'is bunk.' 'Examinations', says the undergraduate, 'are also bunk.' To some extent he is right. Examination questions are unreal and unrelated to life, and are looked upon as an unwelcome imposition. A student will assiduously attend classes, make notes and do private study. The examination he looks upon as completely separate; he will attend to it at the last possible moment. He is like a runner in the 5000 metres who walks all the way to the bell and then tries to make up lost time by running the last lap like a 100 metre sprint finalist — not a good technique, as you can imagine.

Of course examinations are unreal; they are a contrivance whereby the student has the opportunity — usually over periods of three hours — to show how he can tackle fresh problems using the basic knowledge that he possesses. That the questions bear only a slight resemblance to the problems encountered in real life is irrelevant. After all, chess is unrelated to real life, but it certainly tests intelligence and ability. However, there is one vital difference: in the examination game the examiner is not your opponent. He is delighted when your system of study and preparation checkmates the standards set by the College and allows you to progress. Beat the system!

Examination questions should be answered with the skill that marks out a good chess player. Ensure that any answer you give is an elegant work of art; the subject matter of the question will be related to your own studies, but the way in which it should be answered is more related to chess. The examiner is probably an old hand at the game. He appreciates a good attempt at an answer even if the final result is not 'correct'. The knowledge that you possess must be displayed so as to show the examiner that you have the capacity of logical thought and can build further on your present state of development and knowledge. When the examiner looks at your written answers, he does not expect to find evidence of great original skill or perfection; he is interested in your powers of argument, deduction and logical exposition.

By now you will be quite sure that we are 'crackers' — 'elegant works of art' indeed. *You* know quite well how to sit examinations without any guidance, and you have no intention of following anyone's advice. You see, we know you quite well. But read on.

Techniques Are of Vital Importance

You would not have reached your present stage if you had been lacking in ability. Most failures in examinations are due not to a deficiency of knowledge but chiefly to lack of familiarity with the techniques of playing the examination game. One candidate, for example, apparently has a full knowledge of the topic but fails the examination. Another seems to know much less but can pass, and may even show a reasonably acceptable standard. To the uninitiated this may seem surprising and unfair, but to those who have been through the mill the situation is very familiar. The message is clear — examination techniques are of vital importance.

Don't Work for Examinations

You should not study *for* examinations. Study rather to understand the subject — following our suggestions in chapters 2 and 4 on studying and note-making — and passing the examination will be assured as a by-product; the examination need hold no terrors for you. Revisions of knowledge and more intensive study towards the end of the course are good insurance, but don't overdo it. If you come to the examination with a brain that is befogged by lack of sleep and gallons of black coffee, you will not do yourself justice. Your friends may look on regular study as unnecessary: we don't agree and we know more than they do. Some of them may succeed in keeping abreast of course-work but will make little attempt to understand what has been presented to them during lectures and tutorial periods. But as the examination time approaches, they have to explode into a frenzy of 'swotting' activity. This is a technique to be avoided: facts learned in this way do not stay with you. Remember also that most lecturers (if they happen to be your examiners) feel a strong revulsion and antipathy when they find their own cherished and 'brilliant' arguments re-presented in a bowdlerised fashion from inadequate notes and a poor flogged memory. Examiners are searching for originality of approach, for critical judgement and for comparative

With brain befogged by lack of sleep and gallons of black coffee

arguments, all of which can be developed only by a long mental soak in the subject. So remember — study to learn the subject; do not merely work for the examination.

Techniques 'at the Bell'

If you have planned and carried out your strategy of study over the earlier laps, like the 5000-metre runner, you should be on the inside lane and in a good position at the bell for the last lap. The earlier chapters on the techniques of study should be your mainstay up to this point. There are techniques of study during the year, techniques 'at the bell' and techniques on E-days. The more these techniques are made to be routine and intuitive, the greater your chance of being ahead in the last sprint.

You should be on the inside lane and in a good position at the bell

'At the bell', which is somewhere in the region of two months — not weeks — before the date of the examination, you should start to work up your pace gradually and comfortably towards the final three-hour tests. The hours of the examination are not something distinct and separate from the rest of your preparation, but are more like the final short sprint to the tape. Work during the examination is a development of earlier work and a logical culmination of your strategy.

Techniques 'at the bell' are four

    (1)   living with the headlines and main outlines of your subject by the use of *swot cards*;

    (2)   rehearsing old papers (or papers concocted from textbook examples) under examination conditions, with the deliberate aim of making these conditions so familiar that you will be at ease — with the 'this-is-old-hat-to-me' feeling — in the examination room;

    (3)   listening with a much more critical ear to your tutor and to the lecturer — especially if he is also the examiner;

(4)   obtaining familiarity with the types of question which have been consistently set in the past, and making a tentative guess at the likely questions for your examination.

Swot Cards

Reference is made in chapter 4 to the value of making good notes but, as the time of the examination approaches, it is good policy to transfer key facts and figures on to *swot cards*. Under the present examination system, where a good memory is of real assistance, it is necessary to commit these facts to memory, and this is where the swot cards help. They can be carried round in the pocket and referred to frequently — on the bus, while taking the dog for a walk, while shaving, almost anywhere. Use ordinary white postcards, or 5 in. × 3 in. index cards, and coloured pencils for major and minor points, for grouped facts and memorable principles. Do not hesitate to throw a card away after rewriting it in a better form. In fact, the more you re-write them the more valuable the cards become and the less you will need to rely on them.

Swot cards can be referred to almost anywhere

Rehearsal

The astronaut is not launched into space without many months of simulation of the conditions he will encounter. The pianist due to play a concerto in public spends many hours in practising the techniques of using his instrument that the piece requires. He also practises simpler exercises not related to the concerto but contributing, by continual repetition, to the skill which will be at his command on the concert platform. The student taking a written examination, however, very often has only the most rudimentary knowledge of the skills necessary in writing down his thoughts rapidly and accurately and in mastering the subtle techniques of being a successful examinee — techniques that have no connection at all with the amount of knowledge he may possess.

Thousands of students annually attempt important examinations without any practice at all! In presenting yourself to the examiner, the skill with which you save time over small routine items can be very much in your favour, and this skill comes only with practice. It is important, therefore, that you should practise the sitting of examinations in the privacy of your own room, but in conditions that closely simulate those of the examination hall. Many failures in examinations are due to the unfamiliarity and strangeness of the situation. This strangeness induces nervousness and jeopardises the candidate's chance of success. When you sit down in the examination room with the usual small table in front of you, the situation should be familiar and comfortable from the long practice you have carried out. Familiarity conquers nervousness.

Practice in simulated examination conditions must not be delayed until close to examination time. During the year when you have essays to write or problems to solve as part of the requirements of the course, work on a small space on your desk with the items that you are allowed to take into the examination room. Find out what is permitted, for you must simulate the final conditions as closely as possible. Make a list of the permitted aids and make sure that they are all in working order. Even on important occasions, we have known students come to an examination with a fountain pen only partially filled. Precious time in the middle of the writing period was required to find ink and fill the pen. If you use ball-point pens remember that they too run out or refuse to function: test them before use and take a bundle of them to the examination or the practice session.

The basic physical aids to good examination techniques are the following

(a) a watch (showing the same time as the examination room clock!)
(b) a stop-watch capable of registering up to 30 minutes
(c) several sharpened pencils, both hard and soft (2Bs should always be carried and harder ones can be used for more delicate sketching)
(d) a bunch of coloured pencils or coloured ball-point pens
(e) a pencil sharpener
(f) a pen with which you are familiar and which is comfortable to the hand.

These tools and any others that you may need and are permitted for specialist work should also be on the desk at the time of your practice 'examination'. They should always be placed in the same positions each time; you should be able to put your hand on any of them at a moment's notice: no scrabbling around! The watches should lie in front of you, in full view. The other items should be kept in the lid of a cardboard box or in some other receptacle so that they are not pushed off the edge of the table, which is usually quite small.

At first pay little attention to timing, but, as you become familiar with various aspects of your subject, set yourself questions to be answered in a continuous and timed session without reference to any but the permitted aids. Allow a maximum of 30 minutes per question (if it is a 6-in-3-hours paper), using your stop watch so that you do not need to remember the time you started.

As you come within two months of the examination period you should try to answer a complete past examination paper under your simulated conditions, which, by now, should be so familiar that all trace of tenseness and nervousness will have vanished. If your studies have not taken you to the point where you can answer all the questions, answer those that you can and some of them twice. Answering the same question a number of times is a useful exercise in showing how improvements can be made in the way in which you present the facts to the examiner. When the period is over, critically examine what you have done as if you were looking at someone else's efforts. You will be surprised at how much improvement you can find in your technique of sitting examinations from one week to another.

If you are offered an 'open-book' examination do not heave a sigh of relief, assuming that you need merely take in all your books and your year's notes to be able to succeed. The candidate who brings his whole library to such an examination often fails: the facts that he needs are lost in a multitude of pages. Anyway, questions in such examinations are composed so that answers cannot be lifted from your library! The preparations for an 'open-book' examination should rather consist of preparing adequate notes — possibly in swot-card form — of all aspects of the work, with, perhaps, the support of marked passages in a few textbooks.

Listening to the Lecturer

If the lecturer is also known to be the examiner, he is unlikely to set a question on a topic that he has not covered or referred to in his lectures — although this cannot be guaranteed. The examiner is quite entitled to set questions on any topic in the syllabus regardless of whether a lecture on it has been given or not and you should look out for the 'old foxes'. However, by careful listening to your lecturer you may possibly identify his preference for certain topics. Certainly, by engaging to the full in tutorial sessions you can identify the way in which he likes views to be put forward. Tackle all the tasks set during tutorial sessions and know them thoroughly, since it is possible that you might find one or two similar questions in the examination paper. You would also be wise to listen attentively and watch every move in the lecturers' end game. It is very important for you to attend the last two or three lectures of the course. Occasionally a lecturer engrossed in his subject finds that he has concentrated too much on his favourite bits and has not covered all the topics in the paper. He then feels that, in all fairness, he must give some guidance on the loose ends, even at the last moment. Even lecturers and examiners have human feelings. They tend to be kind and wish to give the candidates as much help as they can, although there is no compulsion on them to cover every detail of the syllabus.

What Questions Will Be Set?

Syllabus and content of examination paper go together and it is well to establish your facts about *syllabus* and *questions*. These facts guide the course of your revision. First find out how long the present syllabus has been in force and try to obtain for yourself as many past papers as possible set to that syllabus. Go through all the old papers in detail and construct a table on the following lines.

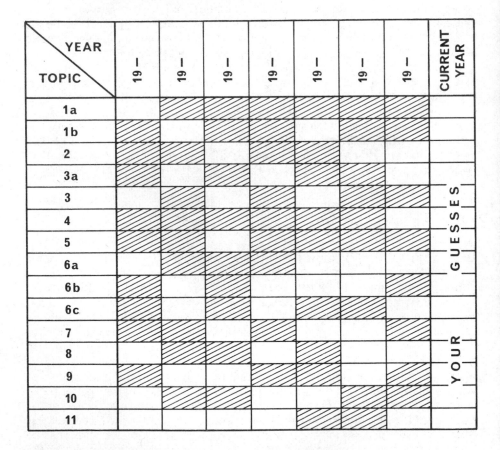

From this you can identify the trends and thus assign probabilities to the various types of question likely to appear on the next occasion. If you were preparing for the paper to which the above chart refers, it would obviously be very foolish to enter the examination without a very full understanding of topics 1a, 4 and 5 (six years out of seven), but it would be equally foolish to assume that you need pay no attention to 11 (two years out of seven). You must bear in mind that you are dealing only with probabilities and — who knows? — the examiner may have been changed next time. You should have studied all the syllabus, but it would be prudent to have a full knowledge of the topics with a high probability.

Assign probabilities to the various types of question

Having said this, it is worth while letting you into a secret — few examiners, in fact, work out any of the topic frequencies and decide either to fill in where the lines in the table are thin or to repeat a question on the 'dead certs'. More often, the examiner finds the day approaching when he must commit his paper on its first stage towards the printers and writes questions as they occur to him. He may have some that he did not use last year, or he may have become interested in a topic in the syllabus that has been given a new twist by some research (perhaps his own). Whereas it is sound policy to prepare a probability chart, never rely on it heavily.

E-day Techniques

Regardless of nerves (which should have been largely removed through practice examinations), resolve to follow a fixed routine during the examination. This makes for the most efficient examination technique. A mnemonic helps considerably in recalling the routine on the appointed day. You will find that the initial letters of the routine operations to be undertaken during an examination form the word

ARTICLE

Memorise what each of the seven letters represents and run through the check list both during rehearsals and on E-day. The steps are

A: Administration
R: Reading through the paper
T: Timing
I: Individual questions
C: Correction and co-ordination
L: Last Minute checks
E: Elimination

Efficiency in tackling examinations comes chiefly from routine practice and all the steps should be followed during the practice sessions.

A: Administration

There is little point in writing an excellent script if it fails, through your own fault, to be processed in such a way as to give you full credit. You are usually given, at the time of taking the examination, a list of printed instructions. These may appear on the question paper, on the answer books (scripts) or on a separate sheet. Whatever form they take, it is absolutely essential that they should be obeyed to the letter. They are all based on long experience of examinations of the type concerned, and ensure that your paper is efficiently marked. The examiner's work will be hampered and your chances jeopardised if any of these instructions is ignored or obeyed incorrectly.

For example, you are often asked to write down the numbers of the questions answered *in the order in which they are attempted.* It is surprising how often this simple request is ignored and the spaces left blank or the numbers put down in any order but that asked for. Don't lose pawns in the game for no good reason! The request is made so that each question can be marked throughout the whole pile of scripts in one operation, before the next question is examined.

When the examiner picks up your script to look for question 5, for example, he ought to be able to open the book at roughly the right place and find question 5. If he cannot do this quickly — either because you have not told him what questions you have answered, or because you have indicated them in an order that is not that in which you have attempted them — he is likely to be mildly annoyed. This annoyance should not influence his judgement, but why take the risk? There is no doubt that the candidate who assists the examiner by carrying out the administrative instructions given to him creates a good impression. The facts that you are asked to record — the number or name of the examination, the number of the seat that you occupy, your address and so on — should all be recorded carefully and completely, even if they seem unnecessary to you. You don't have to mark the paper!

R: Reading through the Paper

Many consider this check a waste of time, but experience has shown that — provided you have studied effectively — the sub-conscious mind works on the problems after you have read them through. Even if, at first reading, you find them formidable, when you come to answer them you will be surprised that they become much easier than you had imagined. So allow ten minutes for a careful and thorough study of the paper, reading every word and phrase with attention. A great deal of effort has been put into making sure that what the examiner requests has been clearly and unambiguously stated. Only answers to what has been asked are of any value. No marks are given for superb answers to questions that you have invented!

Decide which questions you are going to answer and put them in order of difficulty with the easiest coming first. By easiest we mean the one on which you think you can achieve the highest marks in the allotted time for the question. Write the number in *pencil* on the outside of the examination book so as to serve as a guide to you later. The reason for writing in pencil is that you may change the order. Under stage E make sure that you record the correct order in ink.

T: Timing

In addition to 10 minutes at the beginning for reading the paper there must be at least 20 minutes left at the end for a revision of your work. This is most important. This leaves 150 minutes out of the usual examination period of three hours. Apportion the time remaining among the number of questions to be answered. If there are six questions to be answered, all of equal weighting, then allow 25 minutes for each question. Obviously, if one particular question is compulsory and has for example a weighting of $1\frac{1}{2}$ then you must allocate 50 per cent more time to this question than to the others. Jot down a time-table of the times when you ought to stop answering each question. For example, if the examination lasts from 10.00 to 13.00 hours the time-table for six equally weighted questions would be as follows

Reading	10.00 – 10.10	Q.4	11.25 – 11.50
Q.5	10.10 – 10.35	Q.3	11.50 – 12.15
Q.2	10.35 – 11.00	Q.1	12.15 – 12.40
Q.7	11.00 – 11.25	Revision	12.40 – 13.00

Answer your first-choice question and, if you finish or run out of anything else to write before the allocated time, do not give the extra time to the second question but keep it in reserve for the end of the examination. No question should have more than 25 minutes in a 6-in-3-hours examination. This is where the stop watch is useful. If you have not finished your first-choice question in the allotted time, stop writing and leave sufficient space to finish it later. (This may be one or two more pages.) Move on to the next question, and so on through the paper. The reason for this policy is that it is relatively easy to obtain the first few marks (say 10 per cent) for an examination question. It is essential, therefore, that you attempt the required number of questions, in order to play a winning game.

I: Individual Questions

The answering of each individual question in the time you have allowed must be planned like a military exercise. First, be sure that you know exactly what is required. In some questions the statement of the conditions is deliberately written in a complex confusion. The conclusion that you are required to reach may be announced at the beginning, at the end or in the middle. The facts on which you must build your argument are scattered throughout the statement of the problem in what the examiner thinks is flowing English, but which is sometimes anything but clear.

The first step, therefore, is to write down in a list all of the data that you are given. Sometimes one fact or figure that you may need is not defined: you are expected to know it. It may be that calculation is involved. If so, decide what units you are to use. Next, convert all the data to the chosen group of units. Mistakes made by confusing and mixing units are very prevalent, so this conversion should be the first part of the answer to the question; it should not be done on scraps of paper.

The second step is to write down *exactly* what you are required to answer. Usually these requirements are distributed through the question. Write them down in a list (a), (b), (c), (d). The list of data and converted units and the list of required answers should be part of your exposition to the examiner. This immediately shows him that you have powers of organisation and also permits him much better to follow your arguments.

Remember that you must answer only the questions asked and no others. A common fault into which candidates fall is to assume that the mention of a topic in the question is an indication that the examiner wants to know everything about that *and related subjects*. This is quite wrong, and leads to a tremendous waste of examination time, as well as exasperation in the mind of the examiner — an emotion that the candidate is very unwise to arouse! Answering widely in this way merely leads to several pages of your script being completely disregarded. The examiner is not interested in all that the candidate knows, nor can he give marks for the evidence of this knowledge unless it is directed exactly and specifically to the narrow topic of the question.

Examiners realise that their standard of marking can vary slightly according to the mood they are in, and to the time spent on marking. The usual practice, therefore, is to take each question individually and mark that one question on every script before going on to the next question. The same standard is then applied throughout all the scripts. Here you can see the advantage of having a neat hand and a tidy way of setting out your work. Imagine yourself as an examiner working on a huge pile of scripts in pleasant summer weather when you would rather be playing tennis. If in doubt over the value of the answers provided, wouldn't you tend to be generous to the candidate whose work is neat and tidy and easy to follow? Remember that every mark counts! Do all that you can to make the examiner's task easier — not only by setting out your answers neatly but by identifying each answer clearly. For example, candidates often write the number identifying the question in small figures close to the inner corner of the page, where it is often concealed by the way the examination book is bound. In searching for question 7 for example, the examiner must open the book fully at each page until he spots the small number 7 almost tucked into the binding.

Sometimes the candidates have so little imagination and so little understanding of the work of the examiner that a new question is started at the bottom of the page. Thus the examiner must look at the bottom of the page as well as the top in order to find his way to the new question. All questions should start on a fresh page. Waste paper! You may have as many sheets as you need; ask the invigilator. Here is an opportunity for using not only your imagination but also your coloured pencils. If we assume that you are writing on the *right-hand* page of an examination book or on loose examination sheets, bound at the top left-hand corner, then the identifying number of the question should be *large* so that it is easily seen and should be at the top *right-hand* corner. We would go so far as to suggest that *every* sheet that carries any part of the answer of question 9 ought to marked '9' in colour, the first one being '9 Start' the next '9 Cont'd', and the last one '9 End'. If this were carried out by candidates in examinations, what a boon it would be to those who have to mark the scripts!

Remember in numerical questions to write in your scripts the steps that you go through to arrive at a solution. This is particularly important if you are allowed to take into the examination room a small calculating machine. The reason for this advice is that, if you go wrong but the examiner can identify the stage at which you have gone wrong, he is able to give you the appropriate credit. If you omit to declare the steps and have the wrong answer, he can only give you a zero mark.

Whatever you try to transmit to the examiner in a written examination must be written so that it can be read. This may seem a statement of the obvious, but examiners for universities, colleges and professional institutions are agreed that this very obvious point is not appreciated by the candidates. Quite apart from the misuse of the English language — grammar, spelling, punctuation, paragraphing — there is the paramount problem of legibility. If your work is legible you have already scored one point with the examiner. If it is not legible and consists of a series of private squiggles you have already jeopardised your chances of passing the examination. No examiner who has a pile of scripts in front of him is likely to spend much time trying to decipher an unreadable word or sentence. The answer you gave to the question may have been brilliant and put together in a language marked by brevity and clarity. If, however, the examiner cannot read the words, he cannot possibly give you the credit that should be yours.

It is quite clear that in any examination the examiner has a very short time to spend on any individual question. Perhaps the papers must be examined twice by two different examiners in different parts of the country; the marks must be sent in to the central body by a certain date; there may be not only scores of examination papers but hundreds, each of them containing the attempts of several questions. Simple arithmetic will show that if you wish the examiner to appreciate your answer you must present it to him so that the minimum time is required for reading, assessing and marking. Examiners are bound to react pleasurably (with some benefit to the candidate) when an answer is set out so that a quick and accurate judgement of its value is possible. Clear calligraphy is the first step towards this goal.

C: Correct and Co-ordinate

If you have kept strictly to the time-table we have suggested, you will have at least 20 minutes left when the last question has been attempted. You may well have more, but not less time than this to correct and co-ordinate your results. Some of the questions may be completely answered, some may be nearly but not quite complete and some may have been abandoned half-way. But at least you will have attempted the required number of questions.

If you can do so without getting bogged down, go back and complete those questions that are nearly finished since you are likely to gain most marks in this way. Then proceed to those that have still some way to go and take them at least a little further. Spend your time in the way that is likely to give you the maximum return in marks. If by then you are within five minutes of the end of the examination period don't waste time by writing such fatuous remarks as 'sorry, no time'. Rather, indicate in a few words how the rest of your answer would proceed if you had time. If you are right about procedure you might gain one or two more marks. Finally, proceed in the last few minutes to the last two of the seven stages — L and E.

L: Last-minute Check

Read through your scripts putting in the odd finishing touches and making corrections to your English. Never leave the examination room before the end of the examination except for genuine illness. (Nerves don't count — you shouldn't have them after the practice sessions.) Even if you cannot think of anything else to write, sit there — something might come. While your sub-conscious mind is searching for some final point to include in the margins, go on to the final stage.

E: Elimination

Before handing in your script, make sure that all your unwanted work is crossed out and that all work to be presented is in order. Be careful not to cross out wanted material in the heat of the moment. Make sure that all the question numbers on the front of the paper correspond with the questions that you have answered, and appear in the order in which you have answered them. Finally, if asked to do so, tie all the scripts together so that none goes astray.

Last Words

The increased emphasis on techniques in this chapter has been deliberate. Most college failures stem from utter ignorance of the techniques of study and of being examined. It is seldom lack of ability that brings down a student who genuinely wishes to succeed. The standard required for a pass is not high. What topples the majority of candidates is lack of practised techniques. In no other human activity — from rock climbing to dinghy sailing or playing the trombone — would a participant wade in without practising the methods of performance. The technique of squeezing the last mark out of the examination game (for it is so artificial as to be a game) needs as much practice as mastering the breast stroke or converting a try. Don't waste your chances by an amateur approach to examinations: be a professional, whose professional life depends on techniques studied, argued about and practised.

Attendance

It seems hardly credible, but it happens year after year even after reminders are posted. Candidates actually attend for an important examination in the afternoon when it took place in the morning! After a year or more of preparation, don't miss this last technique: study the *final and authentic* examination time-table. Also, if you are not quite sure where the room is, find it the day before. Attendance at the wrong room is endemic! Mistakes like these could lose you a year — a very costly error.

Think and Act

Think (A): Viewpoint

You don't work for examinations, but to understand the subject thoroughly; success in examinations is a by-product of knowledge and techniques, and the techniques are extremely important.

Think (B): Avoid the Dr Johnson Situation

See chapter 2 and do not look on the last fortnight as the only time to work, even if it does 'concentrate your mind wonderfully'. By then, the techniques of study should have soaked you in the subjects you are studying.

Act (C): Swot-card Technique

Choose a part of one of your subjects and write a *swot card* (see the section on Techniques 'at the bell') of postcard or index-card size. Use headlines and main outlines and a colour code (see the section in chapter 4 on Making attractive pages with punch). Keep your eye on the card for two days and then tear it up. Next day write another card on the same topic from memory. Repeat the recipe with other subjects and sub-topics.

Act (D): Rehearsing

When you start rehearsing old papers (Techniques 'at the bell') two months before the examination, write a swot card of the six physical aids plus any others allowed for your particular discipline. One month before the examination, write a swot card for the E-day techniques (the ARTICLE mnemonic). Give both cards the treatment described in (C).

8
Conducting
Committees

As a successful member of society you will be called upon many times in your career to take part in meetings, both for your employer and for your professional organisation. In your private life also you will take part in a variety of activities — educational, social, political. This, too, will involve committee meetings.

College is the best place to learn the techniques of committee work. If you and your committee make a mistake in college affairs the results are usually not disastrous. If you wait until you are in practice, when decisions have important repercussions, a mistake can be a serious matter. So, while you have the chance, develop skill in committee procedures. Later this skill will serve you well.

There are four levels at which you can join a committee. *First*, there are many societies run under the aegis of the Students' Union. *Secondly*, there are the governing bodies of the Union itself. *Thirdly*, there are the administrative committees of the college, on many of which there are student representatives. *Finally*, there is the Governing Board of the College, of which you might be one of the student representatives. This may sound a magnificent position but, in fact, much better personal experience of the techniques of running a committee meeting can be obtained at the lower levels, because you will have more personal involvement. Within these four categories you have the opportunity of participating in the running of the college and its affairs.

Start, in your aim of gaining experience of running affairs, by joining one of the college societies. Any society will do. You can join a society whose interests are your own: this is clearly your first choice. However, there is a good deal to be said for joining a society whose background is strange to you, or with whose aims you are not familiar or not in sympathy. In such a society you can keep a more detached outlook, and your education will be broadened.

Since your object is to be elected to a committee, for the benefit of the experience it provides, it is probably advisable to join more than one society, but don't overdo it. You will not have time for more than one committee if you serve it properly. You will remain an ordinary member of the other societies, and see and question the work of their committees from the 'floor of the house'.

It is not difficult to obtain a place on a committee. People tend to avoid responsibility and particularly the responsibility of office. You may well find yourself Hon. Secretary or even Chairman before you expect these distinctions. Always accept posts of that kind; the benefit to your education in the running of affairs is enormous.

If you are elected to college committees, do not disdain what appears to be a minor representation. More experience of the day-to-day work of committees is obtained by deciding the cost of a plate of soup on the Catering Committee than by listening to the high arguments of policy on the Governing Board of the college. When you eventually get on to any committee it is surprising how quickly the esteem in which you are held grows when you can conduct yourself with confidence in the meetings. This is a very important chapter — so press on.

Order Please

Meetings are conducted according to rules of debate modelled on the rules used in what is probably the most famous talking shop in the world — the Houses of Parliament at Westminster. These rules have grown up through custom and are not laid down by law. To prevent argument, most organisations decide on the rules of debate that they wish to adopt in meetings. These rules are known as the *standing orders*. Often, they are incorporated into the constitution of the organisation and then become legally binding. All colleges and most Student Unions have their own sets of standing orders.

Typical standing orders for a student body deal with the order of business, the minutes, the selection of speakers, Chairman's rules, speeches and interruptions, motions and amendments, withdrawals and additions, closing debates, adjournments, points of information and order, voting, notice of motions, rescinding a resolution, motions of confidence and what happens when these standing orders are suspended. Do study these. There is not enough space in this chapter to do them justice and standing orders vary from one committee to another.

The Chairman is of Vital Importance

Imagine a football match without a referee to interpret and enforce the rules. Although the match might be colourful to watch, it would hardly be good football. The analogy is clear: just as a referee is necessary to interpret the rules, so a Chairman must guide a meeting.

The first duty of any meeting that finds itself without a Chairman is to appoint one. The term for which a Chairman is appointed — whether for years or for one occasion — does not alter his behaviour at a particular meeting. The success of any meeting depends heavily on the Chairman. Since he is the final authority on the interpretation and enforcement of the rules, the committee members must respect and trust him. They will do this only if he exercises his authority firmly and impartially. Therefore, he must know the rules of debate and be able to keep the meeting running smoothly. He must also be able to keep the debate to the point and maintain a time-table. Yet the members must not feel rushed or denied an opportunity to contribute. The Chairman must also be able to relieve tension between members and sense the best time to bring the debate to a close. Regardless of your personal feelings towards the Chairman, you must afford him the utmost respect in addressing him and obeying his rulings. In the matter of address, the universal practice is the phrase 'Mr Chairman'. If the chair is taken by a woman the same phrase can be used or alternatively 'Madam Chairman'.

A Word in Your Ear, Mr Chairman

So you've been appointed Chairman! Congratulations! Being a sensible person, you will already have studied the standing orders and have resolved to take all your decisions without fear or favour, even if it makes you unpopular. If you are to succeed as Chairman you must be well versed in what the committee's task is supposed to be. This seems self-evident, but many Chairmen, because of pressure of other work, come to meetings less than well prepared. Never do this: always have a meeting with your 'Hon. Sec.' and plan a joint campaign for the next meeting. You should rely on your secretary's advice, but it should never appear at the meeting that you are incapable of conducting the business without constant appeals to the Hon. Sec. At your meetings with him try to predict what certain committee members will say and how they will act. There are many types of committee member. Here are some of them. Get to know them.

Try to predict what committee members will say and how they will act

The Know-all doesn't, at heart, see the need for any discussion at all. Why not leave the decision to him — he knows better than anyone else. Because of this, he frequently tries to answer questions addressed to the Chairman.

Quietly but firmly interrupt him, and answer the question yourself; or alternatively, deliberately ask someone other than Mr Know-All to answer it. You can't cure this type but you can keep him in order.

The Shy One hardly ever speaks, partly due to nerves but more usually because he thinks more slowly than his colleagues, and by the time he has thought out a contribution someone else has already said it. Try to recognise this man early in the meeting and, when an item comes up on which you know he has some expertise, ask him for his opinion. Bolster up his ego a little by saying: 'I know you have had some valuable experience on this, Mr S., and the meeting would welcome your advice.' Having broken the ice, the shy one then feels more confident to contribute on his own later.

The Tongue-tied, a type that you will occasionally meet, has some very good ideas but cannot express them clearly. There is a danger that he could become a joke with the other members. Don't encourage this, but rather help him by summarising and re-phrasing his contribution in a gentle and inoffensive way.

The Bore likes to hear the sound of his own voice and jumps into each debate at the earliest opportunity, whether he has anything to offer or not. If he becomes too much of a bore, deliberately choose others to speak rather than him. You can say: 'I would like to open up this discussion and involve members of the meeting who have not spoken much so far.' Alternatively, you can start a discussion by asking someone just beyond the offender to speak first and then go round the meeting leaving him until last.

The Interrupter must be kept under control. If a member interrupts another unnecessarily you should intervene immediately and state that the first speaker has the floor. If the interrupter persists you should deal with him severely or the discussion will become disorderly. Having said that, however, there are occasions when an interjected remark may be helpful or humorous. On these occasions the Chairman is wise to turn a deaf ear to the interruption.

The Chatterbox, although he is not as bad as the interrupter, is still a nuisance. He sits whispering to his neighbours while someone else is speaking in the debate. There is a most effective way to deal with this man. If you are confident that he has been so immersed in his chattering that he hasn't a clue what has just been said, turn to him and say: 'A very interesting point has just been raised; what is your opinion, Mr C.?' Enough said.

The Rambler goes on and on, and gets off the point. Wait for a suitable moment and say: 'That is a very interesting point you have raised, Mr R., which we might wish to take up at a later meeting, but I really don't think it helps our problem at the moment.' Then turn to another member and ask him if he has any 'relevant' ideas.

The Thick One may be one of two kinds: there are those who are genuinely 'thick' and those who pretend to be. Provided they don't hold up the meeting too often, it is often useful to have one such man at the meeting, since he can be relied upon to ask the naive question that many others would like to ask but dare not. Our advice is — tolerate him.

Remember that you are in charge of the meeting and have the ultimate authority. But don't demonstrate your authority unless you have to. Try persuasion, humour, tact and only use the ultimate authority as a last resort.

Conduct of Business

At your preliminary meeting with the Hon. Sec. your main task is to establish the order of business. The secretary will have made a first draft of what should be debated and the main items are probably well defined.

There are, however, preliminary items and also at least two others that normally come at the end. The Agenda paper will be of the following form.

AGENDA

1. Apologies for absence.
2. Minutes of previous meeting
3. Matters arising from the minutes
4. Notice of 'Any other business'
(5.–X. Main items of debate)
Y. Any other business
Z. Date of the next meeting

As you see, there are six auxiliary items, and these are dealt with as follows.

(1) The Hon. Sec. reads the names of those who have sent apologies for absence. Other apologies may be presented orally at the meeting. All these names will be noted in the minutes of the meeting.

(2) The usual practice is to circulate the minutes of the previous meeting with the agenda. (It is assumed that members have read them.) If minutes have been circulated the Chairman will say: 'May I sign the minutes of the last meeting as a true record?' At this stage any member is free to raise any points concerning the accuracy of the report of what happened at the previous meeting, as recorded in the minutes. He cannot use this as an opportunity *to re-open a debate on any of the topics dealt with at that meeting.* This is very important and any attempt to argue about the content of a minute must be quashed by the Chairman. Only the accuracy of description of a past debate can be challenged. If everyone is satisfied that the minutes are accurate, there is either a general murmur of assent, which the Chairman takes as approval, or, more officially, a member will move that the minutes be signed as a correct record, and the motion is then seconded and carried by a show of hands. The Chairman then signs (and dates his signature) the official minutes, which are kept in an official minute book with the minutes of all previous meetings. Once the Chairman has signed the minutes no one is empowered to alter them in any way. However, if the meeting agrees that the minutes are inaccurate in some respect then the Chairman should correct the minutes in his own hand before signing them. If the

corrections are long or numerous the Chairman should ask the Hon. Sec. to make the alterations and re-submit the minutes. This is seldom necessary.

Sometimes the minutes are not circulated in advance of the meetings and the secretary then has the unenviable task of reading out the minutes to the meeting before the Chairman puts the question with regard to accuracy. This is a tedious process and to short-circuit the boredom you will often find someone eager to move the motion: 'That the minutes of the previous meeting be taken as read.' Although this procedure speeds up the meeting, the dangers of such a course of action should be realised. If by any chance there are errors in the minutes, then by accepting such a motion you are authorisng the Chairman to sign the minutes complete with the errors as the correct record of the previous meeting. Remember that these signed records will be legally binding on the meeting!

(3) Further discussion of items from the minutes of the previous meeting is now permitted, provided that the items are not on the Agenda for the current meeting. The 'further discussion' usually takes the form of a report from the secretary, or from a member of the committee, on action taken since the previous meeting. This part of the meeting can take a large proportion of the time available. The time can be shortened, however, if those members who were supposed to make some enquiry or obtain some information, or to write a short factual statement, have not only done so but have informed the Hon. Sec. that it has been done. See the section on Feedback, later in this chapter.

(4) It is advisable to have this item on the Agenda, although it is not always there. If the introduction of 'Any other business' is left until Y, many members of the committee who did not know what was coming up, may have had to leave, especially if the Chairman is ineffective. Therefore, at the end of 'Matters arising' a brief announcement by a member that he intends to raise some item — no discussion allowed at that stage — helps everyone when A.O.B. is reached.

(Y) If a really important item appears in A.O.B. the Chairman should cut discussion short and ask for the problem to be put down as a main item for the next meeting.

(Z) This is a useful addition to the Agenda and gives the first intimation to members that they should book the date. There is usually a flutter of diaries and the Hon. Sec. knows that he has made a step towards a quorum on the next occasion.

Quorum

In the early days of administering justice in England, the King's Commission appointed magistrates. Certain of the magistrates were nominated to a special inner group, some of whom had to be present if a session of the magistrates' court was to be lawful. The name given to his group of magistrates was *quorum*, meaning 'of whom'. Gradually over the years the term has come to mean the minimum number of members who must be present if the meeting is to transact business. Each organisation or society is free to decide what shall constitute a quorum at its own meeting but, when a number or proportion has been decided, it is incorporated into the standing orders and becomes binding at all future meetings. For student committees a quorum would rarely be less than one-third nor more than two-thirds of the members entitled to attend.

The first task of the Chairman at the beginning of any meeting is to decide if there is a quorum present. If so, the meeting can proceed; otherwise, the usual practice is for the meeting to wait a maximum of 15 to 30 minutes for a quorum to assemble. If after this time a quorum is still not present, the meeting must be adjourned. The quorum rule also applies throughout the whole time the meeting is in progress. If, through the premature departure of members, the number present falls below the quorum level the attention of the Chairman should be drawn to the fact; the Chairman then has no option but to adjourn the meeting immediately. Where no quorum is laid down in the standing orders, common sense must prevail even if, legally, there is nothing to stop one member continuing with the business!

Get Moving

It is a cardinal rule in formal debate that no discussion at all takes place until a motion has been proposed, seconded and accepted by the chair. Discussion is allowed only on the motion before the meeting. However, in the committee meetings with which you will be chiefly concerned, the discussion will often be more relaxed and informal. Discussion will usually be allowed before a motion is proposed, although the formal ruling is the safest course for the Chairman to adopt. To make progress each member is allowed to speak only once on any motion that is before the meeting unless he is given special permission by the Chairman.

The Motion

A motion that has been moved and seconded must be accepted by the Chairman, unless it is frivolous or illegal, or covers the same ground as a motion on which a decision has already been taken in the same meeting. The Chairman then reads out the motion known as the *original motion* to the meeting so that everyone is clear as to what the motion is. When the motion has been put from the chair it is then open for debate. Only one person at a time may speak, and he must confine this remarks to the motion before the meeting. Only one motion can be before the meeting at any time. Anyone who wishes to contribute must catch the Chairman's eye and the usual practice then is for the Chairman to call on the persons in the order in which he has seen them. However, the Chairman is within his rights to take contributors out of order if he thinks that the debate will benefit by this.

Once the debate has finished, and before a vote is taken, the mover of the motion has a right of reply to the discussion. He is the only member allowed to speak twice to the same motion. In the reply he is not allowed to introduce any new matter and must confine himself to replying to the points made in the discussion and to summarising the main arguments he put forward when moving the motion.

The Amendment

During the debate, a member who thinks that the original motion could be improved is at liberty to move an amendment, provided that he has not previously spoken to the motion. If the amendment is seconded by another person who has not spoken on the original motion, the Chairman must accept it as a new motion, subject to the provisos that the amendment is not a simple negative of the motion; is relevant; does not cover ground that has been dealt with under a previous amendment; and is not frivolous nor illegal. When the number of members on the committee is small, it may be difficult to abide by the proviso that the amendment must be seconded by someone who has not spoken on the original motion, and in that case common sense prevails.

In formal debates only one amendment may be before the meeting at any one time, but it is common practice in committees to allow several amendments to be moved, seconded and accepted. Normally, the Chairman will take first the amendment that attacks the concept of the original motion and then those that concern minor changes. If all the amendments are lost, one by one, a vote is then taken on the original motion just as if there had been no amendments moved at all. However, suppose that an amendment is carried. A new phrasing is now adopted and displaces the original motion, which is lost for ever. The amended motion takes the place of the original motion and becomes the *substantive* motion.

The Chairman must always put the final substantive motion to the vote. This puzzles some people but the reason becomes clear in the following example. Suppose that a student council was allowed by law to donate money to a political party. Assume that the original motion was to donate £30. The amendment is to donate £15. You may feel that the council should not give any money at all to a political party, but you cannot move an amendment that no money be given since this is a simple negative of the original motion. Therefore if the council is going to give some money, you would prefer it to give less rather than more. In the circumstances, therefore, your first aim is to make sure that the original motion is defeated, and you vote for the amendment. When the amendment is carried, it becomes the substantive motion and when it is put to the vote you vote against it since you would prefer to give nothing rather than £15. This may look as if you had changed your mind — but, of course, you have not. This example illustrates the necessity of always putting the substantive motion to the vote. Once the motion is voted upon and has been carried, it becomes the *resolution* of the meeting. (Note the distinction between motion and resolution.)

The Vote

Frequent reference has been made to a vote being taken and for a majority of meetings this will be by a show of hands for and against the motion, the Hon. Sec. and Chairman being responsible for the counting. For a more important vote, or if it is requested by a member of the meeting, a ballot can be taken instead. This is more time consuming; on the other hand it has the advantage of being secret. The voters mark their preference on pieces of paper, which are returned to the scrutineers appointed by the Chairman or the committee. Sometimes the Chairman and secretary act as scrutineers.

When a vote is taken and everyone votes for the motion, the motion is said to be passed unanimously. On the other hand, if anyone abstains but no-one votes against it the motion is passed *nem. con.* — with no-one contradicting. Incidentally if you misunderstand the motion and vote the wrong way there is nothing you can do about it later to correct the mistake — you have to live with it!

Unless otherwise laid down in the constitution, the Chairman is considered to be a full member of the meeting and, therefore, has a vote that he can exercise as the other members do. If he doesn't abstain, however, he must use this vote at the same time as everyone else. He cannot leave it until after the ballot has been declared. Sometimes a vote results in a tie and to resolve the deadlock it is generally accepted, and often laid down in standing orders, that the Chairman has a casting vote in addition to the regular vote he may have. Although he is free to use this vote in any way that he chooses, it is commonly accepted that he should vote to maintain the *status quo.*

The Chairman has a casting vote in addition to his regular vote

The Role of the Honorary Secretary

The unpaid job of being Hon. Sec. is a demanding one but, as we said above, you should accept this post when it is offered, for it gives you invaluable experience in committee work. Preferably try to be an Hon. Sec. before you are a Chairman. You will then be aware of how the Chairman's efficiency affects the work of the committee.

Calling a Meeting

As Hon. Sec. you are responsible for calling the meeting. Never assume, especially when your members are students, that the committee will assemble without activity on your part. It may have been clearly stated at the previous meeting that the date of the next meeting would be so-and-so, but this will not prevent people from forgetting all about it. So post a notice or send out agenda slips, whether your constitution demands it or not. And no small and indecipherable writing! Post a notice as large as is allowed, with coloured lettering, or mount it on a jazzy or tartan paper. Make sure that it is seen.

At the Meeting

We write this section with feeling, having suffered at the hands of indifferent members of committees.

(1) Make sure that the committee starts its business promptly at the time announced. If a member arrives a minute late, you should be well into the business. This will at least partially ensure a punctual attendance next time. As Secretary, make sure in advance that there will be a quorum present by seeing members of the committee individually and getting them to turn up promptly. If there is no stated requirement for a quorum, persuade the Chairman to start at the advertised time even if only you and he are present. Nothing slows the work of

Have with you all the papers to which reference may be made at the meeting

committees more than dilatory starts.

(2) Provide the Chairman with a note for each item of business, giving him the previous history of the discussion and indicating not the decision but at least the possible decisions that might emerge from the current meeting. Make sure that he has in front of him the names of new members of the committee, so that he can welcome them. If the committee is entirely new, suggest to the Chairman that each member should stand and introduce himself, giving name and representation. Finally, have with you all the papers to which reference may be made at the meeting.

(3) If you are wise, you will have written the minutes of the previous meeting in such a way that the action to be taken on each item is recorded against it. Never use the passive voice. An entry such as, 'It was decided that . . . should be done,' always results in the overloaded Hon. Sec having to carry the burden of action. Rather say, 'At the next meeting, Ms Smith will report on the action taken'; or 'Mr Jones will carry out the instructions of the committee and report back.' Your aim at the next meeting is to make sure that the committee remembers what Ms Smith or Mr Jones should have done. For this reason alone, it is wise to advise the Chairman not to accept a motion 'that the minutes be taken as read'.

(4) Under 'Matters arising from the minutes', an efficient Chairman will turn to Ms Smith and Mr Jones and ask for their reports. If they stammer and say they have not had time, the Chairman smiles icily and says that the committee fully understands and is sure that the reports will be available at the next meeting. He is almost certain to be right! Sharing the work round the committee members can be strongly influenced by the Hon. Sec. in his whispered suggestions to the Chairman, or his invaluable notes slipped along the table.

(5) The setting up of *ad hoc* sub-committees (committees set up for one purpose only and disbanded after their task is accomplished) is a useful technique to make sure that the Hon. Sec. is not left with everything to do. We recall the occasion of a large conference of about 3000 delegates, when the General Hon. Sec. set up many *ad hoc* sub-committees for relatively simple jobs. He was then sure these jobs would be carried out. Never give a sub-committee a complex task; rather split the job into several items, managed by other small sub-committees. On the occasion in question there was, for example, a formally appointed *Lavatory Sub-committee*. This was a small group of people who appointed their own chairman and secretary, and whose task was to see that the signs LADIES and GENTLE-MEN were posted at all the appropriate places in the many buildings used by the conference. They were also given the job of erecting direction signs to the nearest lavatory in corridors

and at the exits to lecture rooms. This sub-committee had nothing else to do and the members carried out their task well: the delegates were all comfortable!

(6) Noting how the committee is proceeding is made more or less difficult according as the Chairman is less or more efficient. You can guide him a lot, but resist all temptations to take over his job by talking to the committee. (If the Chairman is poor you will need lots of control!) Pass notes instead — you will be at his elbow. The more formal the meeting, with motions, amendments and voting, the easier will it be for you to record the discussion and conclusions. Informality is the enemy of the Hon. Sec.

After the Meeting

Your notes taken during the meeting form the basis for your formal minutes to be read at the next meeting. No one interferes with this part of your job! You are expected to produce an immaculate record on your own. In writing the minutes, which should be done the same evening if you wish to avoid mental stress, the general tenor of the debate, as well as its conclusions, should appear. Be sure to record unanimous and *nem. con.* votes as special cases of motions being successful. Remember to note the names of those asked to be responsible for work to be carried out before the next meeting, and make sure that they are clearly displayed in the minutes. Most college committees leave far too much to be done by the Hon. Sec. although sometimes this is his own fault for failing to delegate tasks to others. Often he is afraid that these jobs will not be done, or not done as well as he would do them. His fault here is that he has not organised enough feedback.

Feedback

The definition of feedback that concerns you as Chairman or Hon. Sec. is: *the return to a point of origin of evaluative or corrective information about an action or process.* All organisation succeeds in its purpose in proportion to the effectiveness of its feedback. This is seldom recognised sufficiently by college organisers, such as Chairmen or Hon. Secs.

When some action, decided on in committee, has been carried to completion, the 'evaluative or corrective information' must be returned *as soon as possible* to the secretary of the committee. Instead of trying to do everything himself, the Hon. Sec. should rather arrange for a pattern of feedback that will keep him continuously informed of actions taken. It is often quite unacceptable to wait until the next committee meeting for a report on what has been accomplished by Ms Smith and Mr Jones. There may be further steps which must be taken, after they have completed their tasks and before the next committee meeting.

A good Hon. Sec. should always be aware of the ramifications of his feedback network, and should instil into his committee members the imperative need for sustained communication with the source of origin — the officials of the committee. When a task has been accomplished, a report on this fact must at once be fed back into the system. If a member of a committee receives a letter asking him to carry out some job for the committee between meetings, he must feed back the information that he will do this and, when he has done it, the information that he has done it. You may think that all this is not required, but you are wrong: good feedback prevents error.

Think and Act

Think (A): Viewpoint

Your aim is to be appointed to a society committee or a committee of the Union. The experience is very valuable as part of your education.

Think (B): Knowledge Is Power

Know the standing orders and the duties of the Hon. Sec. and Chairman.

Act (C): Breaking Yourself In

Before you succeed in becoming a member of the committee, take notes at one of the ordinary meetings of the society and write the minutes of that meeting as you imagine they should be.

Act (D): Feedback

Jim has decided it would be a good idea if he took Sylvia to a dance that has been advertised, and he hopes that George will bring Mary. As you start the action, Jim is the only one who knows anything about it. Write down the communications and feedback necessary to make sure that everyone knows the details of the dance, where they are to meet, etc., and that everyone knows that the others know. Mark each communication J to S, or G to M or S to M and give a brief word or two about what the communication contains. Mark each T, L, P — telephone, letter, personal. Remember that there must be something in writing for each; no one is trusting memory.

9
Speaking in Public

A team of market researchers asked nearly 3000 people in the United States what things they feared most. To general surprise, it was not being physically attacked or going bankrupt, but the ordeal of *speaking before a group* which rated the highest vote of 41 per cent. Things like financial problems (22 per cent), sickness (19 per cent), dogs (11 per cent), loneliness (14 per cent) and bugs (22 per cent) were the chief fears of much smaller numbers.

Students are excellent conversationalists in the Students Union bar but ask them to say exactly the same thing in the same way from a platform to a group of people in a hall and they are reduced to jelly. They find difficulty in putting over even the most simple ideas in a coherent way. You are no exception, are you? Yet if you are to exploit your talents to the full and advance in your chosen career you must overcome your unfounded fears and learn to put across your ideas confidently to your employer, colleagues and groups of people in oral reports and lectures.

Few universities and colleges give training in the art of oral presentation and the unfortunate students are left to pick it up as well they can, assuming of course that they think it sufficiently important. As a result, large numbers never try and are never able to communicate effectively through speech, either during their student days or throughout their professional careers. Cast your mind back to recent 'professional' meetings that you have attended and you will realise that the standard of public speaking can be low even among senior men in the professions.

Now, while this is no doubt regrettable, there is a brighter side to the coin. If so many people are failing to communicate effectively, think of the opportunities that await you. Do not be one of the 41 per cent. If you can communicate well by the time you take up your first appointment, you will find yourself several steps ahead of most of your contemporaries. While they are learning, you can shoot ahead in your career, for your clarity of spoken expression, developed by practice, will give you an advantage. Without doubt the best time to learn public speaking is during your days at college. Look around you and ask yourself who impresses you the most. Isn't it the man who can best put over his ideas? Read on and we will show you the techniques that you need to present your ideas orally to a large group of people. If you become competent in this you will have no difficulties in speaking to your employer or a small group of people.

The Shape of a Speech

There are various ways in which you will have to address groups of people and this chapter concentrates on the easiest — giving a lecture. The following chapter takes you on to a more demanding type of oral presentation — reading a Paper. Later in life, when you become well known as a good speaker with something to say, you may be invited to 'address' an audience. You may not even tell them in advance the title of your talk. Because you have shown yourself to be so fluent, so interesting and so captivating no one questions that your address will be worth hearing. Well, that is a long way ahead and hardly a topic to be covered in this book, so let's come down a step or two.

Any type of speech — lecture, paper, address, and so on — is in four parts — Preparation, Beginning, Body, Peroration: PBBP. Remember that.

The Preparation

Don't be misled into thinking that good speakers speak 'off the cuff' — far from it. The chances are that the brilliant off-the-cuff speech or lecture you heard last week was in fact researched, prepared and practised for weeks in advance. Although from time to time you will be called upon to speak without preparation, your best performance will nearly always be the result of thorough planning. Your ultimate aim is to be able to speak to a large audience and yet make each individual feel that you are speaking to him personally. If you can do that, you will have no difficulty in your professional career with board meetings, meetings with clients, reports to committees or any of the occasions when you need to say merely a few words or talk for an hour.

Some of your most original ideas come in fleeting moments; book them down immediately

Well, let's get down to the work of preparation. By way of example, assume you are to give a lecture on a specific topic. First, collect all the material you need by reading around the subject. Soak your mind in everything that you can find relating even remotely to it. You will know several weeks or months in advance that you have to give this talk. Make a point of jotting down any ideas that come into your head. Some of your most original ideas come in fleeting moments — in the street, in the bath or just before going to sleep. Book these ideas down immediately, otherwise you will forget them, but do not bother at this stage to maintain any sort of order. You will find it a great advantage to carry with you, everywhere, a small pocket notebook or pocket tape recorder for this purpose. You can avoid the bulk of a pocket book by carrying loose post cards, which can be easily whipped out for note-making.

Do not leave the preparation until the last moment. You cannot sit down and think of brilliant ideas to order. They just don't come that way. Nor can you expect to leave all the preparation until the evening before your lecture or speech and then make a success of it. That is the perfect recipe for failure. Often the shorter the speech the longer the early thinking. An after-dinner speech of five or ten minutes may take weeks of preparation if it is to be brilliant and scintillating.

A week or two before you are to give your lecture or speech, immerse yourself in the task of expanding your notes and ideas. First decide what you are trying to achieve and fix that aim firmly in your mind. If you don't know what you want to achieve you cannot achieve it. Are you setting out to teach, argue, entertain or what? Secondly, put yourself in the place of a typical member of the audience. What has he come to hear? What is his level of education? How can you help him? Remember that the audience exists only in your imagination. People sit one by one and react one by one. This is why you must prepare your talk with the individual rather than the whole audience in mind. On another occasion you may be giving a talk on the same subject to an entirely different type of audience. Then you must be prepared to re-write the lecture completely with another individual in mind. This is an exercise in communication, and unless your talk is tailored to the needs of the audience you will introduce a blockage in the line of communication — you will have failed. True, you may leave the audience with the impression that you are brilliant, but what good is that if they understand not a word and are thoroughly bored? We once heard a famous professor of mathematics give a lecture to the local Literary and Philosophical Society. The subject was shock waves — complex and difficult. Putting aside all the mathematical symbols by which he normally described shock waves, he put over his ideas in physical terms that his audience readily understood. As a result, the lecture was a great success. What would have happened had he given the mathematical lecture he normally gave to his students?

With your objectives clearly in mind, and a vision of a typical member of the audience before you all the time, the lecture can begin to take shape. It should follow the long-established pattern of all good speeches — *beginning, body, peroration.* This is the creative part of the work and in our opinion the most difficult. While there are times when the outline of the speech can be drafted quickly, it usually takes many hours of effort to produce an acceptable piece of work. As a start, the outline of the lecture is expanded in the basic parts of *beginning* and *body*. Leave the end or *peroration* until later. The main ideas you are trying to convey to your audience should find their places in this expanded form. Then, by using the ideas gleaned during your researches and already noted, you add flesh to the expanded outline and transform it into a speech that flows well and puts over your ideas in an effective way.

The Beginning

The beginning of the lecture is of vital importance. It should win over the audience to your wavelength. Each member should then be receptive to the important ideas that you hope to put over in the main body of the lecture. The beginning can take various forms — a question or a startling statement that relates to the audience or to the main topic of the speech; an appropriate story, joke, illustration, quotation or a reference to an earlier lecture if you are doing a series. Then plunge straight into your subject without circumlocution. The audience appreciates an expert dive at the deep end.

The Body

The body of the talk or speech should contain the arguments and main ideas that you are trying to develop. Inexperienced speakers generally fall into the trap of trying to pack in too many details, or of choosing a subject that is too wide in content. An audience can absorb only two or three ideas during a lecture. The human posterior cannot sustain the listener on a hard seat for more than about 45 minutes without a serious reduction both in the listener's attention and in the link between speaker and audience.

Inexperienced speakers try to pack in too many details

The speaker who starts by saying, 'This is a vast subject and we can touch on only one or two aspects of it,' has chosen the wrong subject. Your subject must be tightly structured. For examples of wide subjects that cannot be effectively handled in 45 minutes, and of subjects on the same themes that would make interesting lectures, study the following. The first column is the wide and inappropriate subject and the second column the acceptable one.

Topographical surveying	Measurement of distance by radar methods
Scottish traditions	Howtowdie and other Scottish dishes
The Second World War	The fall of Singapore: 1942
The history of flight	Alan Cobham's pioneering flight to the Cape: 1926

The plan you have in mind must be known to the audience. We suggest three sections to the body of the lecture; most subjects can be covered in that number of divisions. Give each of them a title which should be announced after the beginning. A short summary of what you mean to say is then followed by your dive at the deep end, with the first section. Tell your audience when you have come to the end of the first section and give a quick summary of it in about 50 words. Then announce the start of the second section and give its title. When that part is complete, say so, and summarise the first two sections again. Then announce the start of the third and final section by its title and when you have finished summarise the whole lecture once more, repeating — as you should have done several times during the lecture — the main points that you want to ram home.

You may think that this is much too elaborate, but if you want the man in the back row to go home with a good impression of you as a lecturer, and with your three main statements humming in his head, then you must practise repetition and summary.

There was once a Professor Royce of Harvard who was an attractive speaker and who had large and interested audiences both in public lectures and in his instructional classes. A puzzled friend asked Mrs Royce why her husband had such a good reputation. Her reply is well worth remembering and studying. She said

> 'Oh, Professor Royce's method of lecturing is quite simple. He always tells his students at the beginning of the hour what he is going to tell them, and how he is going to tell it to them; then he tells them exactly what he told them he would tell them in exactly the way he told them he would tell them; then at the end of the lecture hour, he always takes time to tell them that he has told them what he told them he would tell them.'

If you consider that visual aids in the form of slides, films or an overhead projector would help you to get over a particular point then incorporate them into your speech at this stage. But only use them if they result in a definite improvement. Never use them as 'crutches' or 'padding'. See the next chapter on the use of visual aids and on the technique of constructing the body of the talk.

To maintain the interest of the audience use anecdotes, incidents, personal experiences and humour, but only if they can be incorporated as a logical and relevant part of the speech. Soon after a graduate took up his first job he was called upon to present a report at a research laboratory. Noticing that his lecture was placed immediately after lunch and that the majority of the audience, who were middle-aged, usually dozed off at this time of day, he determined that he would not lose his audience and inserted an inordinately large number of jokes, some of which were hardly relevant. True, nobody went to sleep, and one member of the audience remarked that he enjoyed the lecture better than a turn at the local variety club. The speaker, however, was quite rightly reprimanded by his superior.

The Peroration

We have now reached the final letter of our mnemonic PBBP. Peroration means 'the conclusion of a speech summing up the points and enforcing the argument'. Having developed your main argument or line of thought in the body of your speech you can conclude it in a variety of ways. Include a brief and succinct summary of the main points made, showing their cumulative meaning. Make a definite appeal for action, or quote a story or personal experience that leaves the audience with something to remember. Now, more than ever, every word must carry a punch.

Techniques in Talking

Remember, during the period of preparation, to visualise the audience and imagine yourself actually speaking the words to individual people. In a general speech or lecture do not be frightened of keeping to simple thoughts and ideas. Students are often terrified of being made to look foolish and consequently pitch their talk at too high an intellectual level. Don't do this or you run the risk of losing the audience. *Always put yourself at the receiving end of your talk. Think of the man in the back row.*

Writing It Up

Until you gain more experience you should now write out your speech in full as you are actually going to say it, not as if you were writing an article or a chapter of a book. You need an entirely different style for an oral presentation. Many boring talks and sermons would make excellent articles to be read at leisure. Similarly, many fine speeches, transcribed verbatim, make poor reading because they contain too few ideas.

Practice Sessions

Well, that's the hardest part over. Although you will modify parts of your written talk during the practice sessions you have now completed the major creative effort and that is always the most difficult part. By the way, in case you think you will be taking the fully written-out speech with you on The Day you have a shock coming. In no circumstances is that allowed: it is a recipe for disaster. Cast your mind back to the papers and seminars that you have heard read from a full text. Were any of them interesting? Very few; the reason is that reading the speech usually prevents a speaker's personality coming over to the audience. Once you have had several years of experience you may be able to read without appearing to do so and to put in colloquialisms – but not yet. You should not even have the full text with you in case of an emergency. Invariably with the onset of nerves you would resort to reading it, so — no full script. But, you might argue, I may not be able to remember all the points accurately. This is not as important as you may think. The majority of people would prefer an interesting lecture that is 90 per cent accurate to one that is 100 per cent accurate but is dully read. Notes must suffice and extra points must be brought out in the discussion after the lecture.

Stand up in a room on your own with your notes on a table in front of you and imagine yourself speaking to the audience. Talk around the notes you have. If a part doesn't sound quite right, try again. Go over and over it and check that you are still keeping within the set time limit. Then borrow a tape recorder and record your efforts. Listen carefully and criticise. Modify and record again. Take special care if you want to emphasise a particular point with a pause. There is no substitute for practice and this can be continued at odd times — while taking the dog for a walk, for example. *It takes a lot of practice in private to be yourself in public.*

Casting Your Voice

Many simply look on the voice as the instrument through which a speaker transfers his thoughts to others. But it is far more than that. It is a sensitive barometer that conveys to the listener an impression of the speaker's personality, his feelings, emotions and attitudes and even the level of his intellect. Often it is far more revealing than we would wish. Because of this, many beginners are particularly fearful. As a result, some speakers over-react to their personality. This is a mistake; usually, the change is very artificial and is obvious to all. The result is that it hinders rather than helps the flow of ideas. Whatever your accent, your aim should be to keep your speech clear, loud, understandable and appropriate to the occasion.

Gestures and Sincerity

A good speaker uses not only words and his voice to communicate — he speaks with his whole body. If he doesn't, there is something seriously lacking in his presentation. Gestures can be as eloquent as words.

The chances are that, if you are animated and alive in your manner during normal conversaion, you will need only a little practice to speak with your whole being from the platform. If, however, you are not naturally expressive, then you will need to practise both in your everyday living and for your public-speaking. To start with, use your gestures to get over some simple meanings. By using your hands you can indicate size, weight, shape, location, contrast or comparison; by smashing your fist on the table you can stress the importance or urgency of the message. But use the gestures only if they convey visually to the audience the same message that is coming over in your words. There is an old story of a caretaker who was dusting the pulpit in a small chapel and came across the notes left by the preacher on the previous Sunday. Glancing down he noticed written in red next to one point: 'weak point — smash fist on hand to give it conviction'. It just doesn't work.

To summarise; your aim should be to put over your message with poise, power and vividness, with eyes bright, hands expressive and conveying the impression that you are vibrantly alive and passionately believe in what you are saying. But above all, be sincere and genuine. If *you* don't believe what you are saying, how can anyone else? But don't repeat the *same* gesture at regular intervals. This can be a distraction to the audience; they may miss what you are saying as they wait for the gesture to re-appear.

Notes

To sound really genuine you must be natural and talk directly to the audience — not to a piece of paper on the rostrum. Indeed, the best speaker will have no notes at all, but this is the ideal and rarely achieved. The majority of good speakers, therefore, manage with a few notes on a single sheet of paper. Some use several sheets or cards but there is a danger in this; the audience may see the speaker turn over the pages. This can be distracting, particularly if the audience begins to concentrate on how many are left rather than on what the speaker is trying to say. In the early stages of practising on your own you will need fairly full notes to refer to, but as your speech becomes more polished you will be able to reduce the number of key words and sentences to fit on to one sheet of paper.

The Presentation

Before you give the lecture or speech, check on the hall or room where you are to speak and see that all the facilities that you need are available. Check the rostrum for height and, if you need them, see that there is a blackboard and chalk and a projector and screen. Go through your slides with the projectionist and check that they can be seen on the screen. Please — no slides with minute writing on a dull background. If there is a disturbing glare from the reading light over the rostrum or a spill of light on to the screen — a common fault — take steps to correct this. Finally, if the hall is large ask someone to check that your voice can be heard clearly at the back.

Right — are you ready to go? Are you dressed suitably for the occasion? Remember you don't want a small point like appearance to cause a blockage in the communication channel at this stage. By the way, don't try to slip the whole written speech into your pocket: notes only please.

On the Platform

You are on the stage now. You take your seat next to the chairman and listen to his introduction. If he is a good chairman his remarks will be brief. He may introduce a little humour and say a few flattering things about you (don't get big-headed — he doesn't really mean it), but he will realise that the audience has come to listen to you and not to him. If, during his remarks or during the early part of the meeting, something particularly relevant has occurred you might try to introduce this into your opening remarks — but don't do it if it is going to disturb your train of thought. Don't worry if you are somewhat nervous. Many famous people who appear regularly before the public still feel nervous just before they begin to speak or perform in some other way. Anyway, you can always console yourself that you have prepared your talk thoroughly and that you know very much more about the topic than the audience does. Whatever your feelings you should now stand up and exude confidence even if you don't have it. This is the first rule

STAND UP CONFIDENTLY

To become accustomed to hearing your own voice it helps to memorise the first few lines of your talk. You will soon be feeling much better and, once the audience responds to the first humorous remark, you will actually begin to enjoy yourself, but you must remember, particularly if you have a weak voice, the second rule

SPEAK UP CONFIDENTLY

Are your knees knocking? Don't worry. No one else can see and we all have that trouble. Look down at the rostrum only as often as is necessary to remind you of the next point in your notes. Look directly at the audience and speak to them. If necessary, choose one or two particular people in various parts of the hall and look at them in turn and speak to them personally. Resist all temptation to hide yourself away in a shell by looking at your feet, or staring over the heads of the audience, or looking out through a window.

Hands are a blessing but can also be a nuisance. What do you do with them? Wherever possible you should use them intelligently to illustrate the points you are making; but remember that over-use can be very annoying to the listener. If in doubt, particularly in the early stages, you should hold them by your side or place them lightly on the rostrum. This will stop you playing with the loose change in your pocket or twisting the top button of your coat.

Legs should provide no problem, and should be kept still and straight — unless you wish, by moving them, to make some particular visual impact. However, nerves do curious things to the legs. Different people are affected in different ways. Some put all their weight on one leg and swing the other like a pendulum; others shift their weight from one leg to another at short regular intervals; and others resort to walking from side to side or sideways and backwards in minute squares. One lecturer we knew actually walked through the audience while continuing his talk. Whatever the nervous habit, it distracts the audience and you must resist it. Aim to keep your body in a restful, natural position.

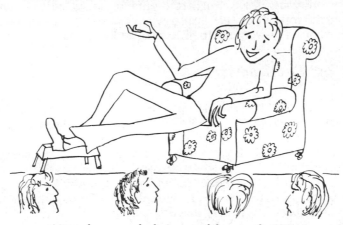

Aim to keep your body in a restful, natural position

Avoid all annoying mannerisms in word or action. These are extremely difficult for the speaker to spot himself and usually they have to be pointed out by others. The difficulty is that there are no hard and fast rules as to what constitutes an annoying mannerism. Whereas a particular habit can be annoying when one person does it, it can be looked upon as an endearing characteristic in someone else — hence the need for honest criticism from a friend in the audience.

As you become more accustomed to public speaking you will become conscious of the feedback from the audience as you are speaking and, although you many not be able to change the content of the speech, you will be able to modify its presentation to meet more nearly the needs of the listeners. Communication is a two-way process and any speaker who ignores the feedback is not communicating: he is just off-loading his ideas.

As you come to the end of your lecture do not drift along to 'finally' and 'lastly' and 'in conclusion'. If you suddenly discover from your notes, or remember, that you have missed one of your favourite points don't say: 'Oh, there's just one other thing . . .'. This breaks the countdown to the final closing of the talk. Keep it for the discussion to follow. When you have presented your final summary obey the golden rule

SHUT UP AND SIT DOWN

You should, of course, be well within your time limit.

Well, how do you feel? How do you think you have done? The chances are that you will feel utterly drained of energy and this is a good sign, since it shows you have given fully of yourself. On the other hand you will probably not be able to remember exactly what you said. Don't worry: this is very common among speakers. Gradually, as you get more practice you will develop more control and eventually you will even begin to enjoy the experience and thrill of speaking in public. Incidentally, if at any time you perform really badly and feel very depressed and decide to pack it all in, remember that you are playing for very high stakes and that everyone who has gone before you will have made the same mistakes that you have made. The men at the top didn't give up, so why should you? Carry on and take every opportunity that you can to give talks and lectures.

Progress and Development

As time goes on and you are able to control your nerves, you will find that you are able to think while speaking on your feet. This means that you are now in a position to try speaking 'off the cuff'. Get practice in this as often and as early as you can. If in doubt have a go — you will nearly always perform better than you think you will; you will improve with practice. You need lots of it, and it is far better to get this as a student than later in life. There are plenty of opportunities for you during debates, question time in class, seminar papers and society meetings. To generate confidence you will find it helpful to memorise a few jokes for standard occasions. This means that when you are called upon to speak at a moment's notice you can quickly modify one of the jokes to suit the occasion. This gives time to think about any other remarks that can be made. Make a point from now on of jotting down all the jokes that you hear at meetings or dinners and keep them in a special file. It is surprising how the number grows and how useful they are, not only for impromptu speeches but also for prepared ones. This applies particularly to any after-dinner speeches you will be called upon to make.

Criticism

In all the advice given so far there has been one major omission — criticism. Although you will improve enormously with practice, you will do it far more quickly if you have friends who are willing to be critical of your performances. You do need this criticism, because as you get your nerves under control you will then concentrate your attention on removing any mannerisms and other annoying habits constituting blockages in the communication channel. How can you remove these unless you know what they are? The difficulty is in finding a friend who is willing to be frank with you.

Practice Makes Perfect

We know of two University departments where the staff provide friendly criticism to undergraduates through a course on Professional Communications. The course covers committee procedures, job applications and the like, but the majority of the time is taken up with practice in public speaking. The class is split into groups of between 10 and 20 and each is led by a professor or senior member of staff. At the first few meetings each student draws from a hat a piece of paper on which is written a topic. He is not allowed to open this paper until 2 minutes before he goes up to the rostrum. He thus has 2 minutes preparation time and then has to speak for 2 minutes on the topic he has drawn. After 1½ minutes have elapsed, an orange light on the rostrum goes on, and after 2 minutes a red light is shown. It is looked upon as a crime to stop talking before the 2 minutes are up. After the presentation, the remainder of the group criticise the student's performance firmly but kindly (knowing that their turn will come soon). The senior members of staff also have to take part and are criticised in turn by the students. Later in the year the proceedings are recorded on tape and played back so that the student can criticise himself. Criticism is levelled both at the content of the speech and, more importantly, at the way it is put over and the use of hands, legs, etc. Later still, a student can choose his own subject in advance and speak on it for 5 minutes, and once again he is kindly but constructively criticised. The progress that can be achieved in a few weeks is remarkable. As a climax to the course there is a series of heats leading up to a grand final, in which there are four competitors. The whole class decides, by using a marking schedule, who should be the finalists. In the final, each competitor has to speak for 2 minutes on a topic he has drawn by lot, and then later for 5 minutes on a topic of his own choosing. The judges on this occasion are three in number and are all from outside the department -- the Vice-Chancellor, a senior member of the profession from outside the University and the President of the Students Union. It is interesting to note that, although several of the students at the beginning of the course objected to its being compulsory, almost without exception they found it to be extremely beneficial and at the end thanked the leaders for having organised it. The value of the course lies in the fact that the students can obtain honest criticism. The authors found that the majority of the students were much better speakers than they originally believed. After a few weeks their colleagues were telling them that they were comimg over well; their confidence then increased. This enabled them to take part in Students Union meetings and debates and to show real confidence.

Fortunately for those readers who are now convinced that there is great personal value in their becoming good public speakers, there is another means of obtaining practice and criticism. In most major towns there are speakers clubs similar to the famous Toastmasters International. These clubs have been formed by people from all walks of life whose sole aim is to improve their own standard of communication. Meetings are organised to give each member the opportunity to practise-off-the-cuff speeches, prepared speeches and the art of chairmanship. Everybody criticises everybody. It is relatively inexpensive and the company is magnificent.

Think and Act

Think (A): Viewpoint

Don't think you are speaking to an audience. You are speaking to a person.
He is in the back row.

Think (B): Knowledge Is Power

Remember that you know a great deal more about the subject of your talk or
lecture than the audience does. If you are nervous — which means that you
are keyed up and will do well — just look them over as you stand up and think
the phrase: 'I know more than you, you poor things!' This works wonders.

Act (C): Practise Cutting Up the Body

Choose a subject that you know well —chess, hockey, bee keeping, knitting,
local accents, tennis — and write out a simple synopsis. Divide your draft into
three main parts and then into three again. Draw a pattern diagram (chapter
4) on a swot card (chapter 7) and keep looking at it for a couple of days. Don't
let it leave your person. Then tear it up and throw it away, and draw another
one from memory. Practise doing this with any subject that comes to mind.
When you have to prepare a lecture, the technique already learnt will make
the job easier.

Act (D): Summaries

Take a subject that you know well and divide it into three main sections,
following the techniques of (C). Write summaries of each of the three parts
(about 50 words each). Then write summaries of parts 1 and 2 together and
then a summary of the whole subject (maybe 100 words this time). Such
summaries must form part of every lecture.

10
Reading a Paper

The curious phrase that forms the title of this chapter comes from the early days of learned societies. These were bodies set up to observe and record aspects of life and nature instead of merely philosophising about them; the first was the Royal Society of London, founded by Charles II in 1662. Members of the Society congregated then, as they do today, to exchange and record observations and ideas, and a member who had something to say would read his contribution from a sheet of paper. These early contributions were often very short and deserved the title, 'A Paper'. If your library has copies of the early transactions of the Royal Society, browse through the pages and you will get a glimpse of those early days of communication based on observation and experiment.

Today, although the same phrase is used, the Paper is usually a much longer and more closely argued affair. But it still carries the hallmark of originality that was the attraction of the early communications. The content of a modern Paper may contain the distillation of researches covering many years of meticulous observation. It may be some new and original interpretation of a controversial topic or it may be a record of some original achievement or exploration.

Sometimes the results of research are printed only. Sometimes they may be given orally to an audience without being recorded in print. This chapter, however, deals with a contribution to knowledge of a standard that is considered valuable enough not only to be printed as a permanent record, but also to be presented orally and defended against argument. *This is a high point of professional communication.*

The Paper is printed by a learned society or some specialist organisation and circulated to the members in advance of the oral presentation so that they have the opportunity to study it in detail before the meeting. The meeting at which the presentation takes place may be an ordinary meeting of the society or perhaps a special conference or symposium but the basic method of presentation is the same. After the author has read the Paper the meeting is thrown open for discussion; this can take the form of questions, arguments or even attacks on the subject matter. But at the end the author has the right of reply, in which he can defend his conclusions. The discussion, along with the printed record of the Paper, then goes into the permanent archives of the society.

This type of presentation involves the organisers in considerable expense, as can be imagined, and only those Papers that have merit are considered for such treatment. If you have the opportunity and privilege of presenting a

Paper in this way, you have not only the honour of the occasion to consider, but also your responsibilities to the body that has invited you to put forward your views. These responsibilities impose restrictions and controls that must be recognised well ahead of the event. Regrettably, the standard of presentation of Papers often fails to match the importance of the occasion and the professional standing of the author. This is due to a lack of knowledge of the techniques that make the presentation of a Paper a skilled and satisfying performance. Although the presenting of a Paper is far removed from throwing the discus, being a concert pianist or acting in a London theatre, the techniques required to obtain a first-class result are just as important, and take as much effort and practice.

Two Papers Not One

If you accept an invitation to read a Paper, you must resign yourself to preparing two Papers — one for printing and one for oral presentation. These are not the same; what is stimulating and informative as a short oral presentation is not adequate for desk study, and what has been written as a carefully prepared desk study will probably cause mental indigestion as an oral presentation.

Papers of the kind that we are discussing here are printed in advance because they are normally of such complexity that their meaning and significance cannot be absorbed by an audience on oral presentation only. The readers need time to check and compare parts of the Paper with each other, to study diagrams and tables and to decide whether your arguments are sound.

The majority of the audience at the oral presentation will probably not have had the time or the inclination to make a full study of the printed Paper. Only those who intend to disagree with you during the discussion will have carefully studied every word and underlined phrases; they may even have written rude remarks in the margins. To them, the presentation of the Paper orally is something of a waste of time; they want to get on to the discussion so that they can have the pleasure of cross-examining you.

Too often the difference between the written and oral presentation of the same matter is not fully appreciated by authors who have not studied the necessary technique. Remember that each of the audience comes clutching his copy of the Paper, read or unread, and he looks to you to put it before him in an interesting way. The oral presentation must have as its first objective the simple illumination of the printed text already in the hands of the audience, but it should also be directed to giving an understanding of your arguments to those who have not read the Paper.

If it becomes clear to the audience that an author is going to read all or portions of his printed text, and show the same diagrams and tables on the screen as appeared in the text, the copies will be brought out from under the chairs and it will be 'eyes down' as at a Bingo game. Your reading of the Paper will be checked by the audience, all turning a page as you do. This type of presentation is far too common and you must avoid it. The only way to do this is to make the oral presentation completely different from the printed text. As soon as it is clear that there is to be no identity between what you are saying and the details of the text, the copies will remain under the chairs, and the audience will give you their undivided attention.

Admittedly, there is a great deal of work involved in writing two Papers, one for printing and filing and one for a short description of your ideas, but the reward in interest from the audience is well worth the effort. The discussion is brighter and more effective, and you will be rated an effective speaker on the subjects in which you have already made some reputation.

Controls and Timing

All the techniques advanced in chapter 9 (Speaking in Public) apply even when you are reading a Paper, but there are further controls and restrictions that make the preparation phase for a Paper a much more demanding task.

Your Paper when printed can occupy only a defined number of pages in the Proceedings of the society, conference or symposium. It will be very unwise of you to expand your presentation beyond these limits, for the editor will only use his 'blue pencil' and cut you down to size. It is much safer for you to plan from the beginning to fit your manuscript to the requirements laid down. It saves a great deal of time, both for you and for the editor. He would be unlikely to cut parts out of the Paper without your agreement, but why deal with such matters twice? Send in the Paper to the requirements of the organisers and retain for the discussion period any gems of information that you have not managed to include. The discussion will usually be printed in the final publication; you will always find it useful to have extra items in reserve when the oral discussion ensues.

If your printed Paper is to contain diagrams, tables or photographs, you must consult the editor. You will have been given a figure for the number of words allowed. It is important to know whether the space occupied by diagrams and photographs must be subtracted from the space allowed for the text. If you have access to copies of previous publications of the same society or conference, you may be able to decide this point by examining previous printed Papers. It is essential that you should adapt what you have to say and show to what is required by the editor. Never write expansively, but cut, trim and adapt until the printed paper fits the pattern. A study of previous Papers will also show you the house-style of the organisation — the way in which text is broken up by headings, for example. Are these headings in capitals, or in bold capitals and lower-case letters? Is there a space between the heading and the text that follows, or are they on the same line? Are the headings followed by a punctuation mark — a colon perhaps? If these and other small points are observed in the manuscript, not only will the editor bless you, but there will be no tampering with your carefully written text, a point of some importance.

You will take much longer to prepare a Paper for printing than you imagine; the mental and physical effort required is demanding, and you must give yourself much more time than you at first consider to be necessary. You will be given a date on which the finished manuscript will be required for printing. Having been at the editorial end of this process, we would impress on you that compliance with this and other controls is a courtesy that you must extend to the hard-pressed secretary of the conference. Apologising and saying that you regret being so late is no consolation to secretaries and editors who must get the printing done before another deadline looms up ahead. If you are given the privilege of reading a Paper, comply with the controls.

Turning now to the controls over your oral presentation, you will find much less interference by the editor or secretary of the conference with what you say and how you say it. But there is one control that you will certainly encounter. You will be given a stated number of minutes in which to make your presentation and to show all the diagrams that you have brought with you. It is the height of selfishness in a busy conference to take more time than you are allotted, yet this is a very common fault. Because organisers recognise that speakers cannot be trusted to watch the clock, elaborate electrical signals — green, amber and red lights — are used. We once saw a speaker go through the whole sequence twice! This showed a barbarous lack of sensitivity, but it is quite common to see the red light burning for some time before the speaker deigns to sit down. The more this control is disregarded, the less time there is for discussion, and still less time for the speakers to reply.

Organisers of conferences often make the mistake of having too many Papers on a given topic in a single session. Sessions are controlled by ingestion of food and drink. The periods breakfast to coffee, coffee to lunch, lunch to tea, and tea to cocktails are often filled with Papers whose presenters disregard the other speakers and occupy too much time. This leads to mental indigestion, even if the physical equivalent is avoided. Find out in advance how many minutes are allowed for your oral presentation; it needs only a little practice to discover how much you can say in that time. Then cut this to 80 per cent to allow for the exigencies of the discussion hall, and the chairman will be your friend! It is always to your advantage to keep back some of your best points for the discussion or for your written replies to correspondence, so *never* overstep your presentation time if your communication is to be skilled.

The Printed Paper

Assuming that you have agreed to comply with the controls laid down, that you will write to the house-style and prepare diagrams in the form required, what are your immediate priorities in writing? As we have said in chapters 6 and 9, you must always imagine that you are writing or speaking to individuals rather than to a mass of people. People react as individuals even when they are together. The person for whom you are writing the printed version of your work is not receiving your statements in the same conditions as he will find during your oral presentation of the same material. To this extent he is a different person when he is reading the reprint of your contribution. He is most likely sitting at a desk, pencil in hand, trying to find points with which he heartily agrees, or with which disagreement is intense. On the other hand, he may not be taking the matter so seriously; he may be lounging in a chair with a glass of his favourite beverage close at hand. The printed version must first contain the full argument that you wish to present, with the evidence on which you base your findings. It must also be clear and precise so that the lounging person will be able to follow the drift of your story. All the techniques put forward in chapter 6 are applicable here.

Diagrams for Printing

Most Papers require some support to the text by means of diagrams giving numerical, historical, social or other data in graphical form. Each diagram in the printed paper may carry several ideas or illustrations of trends, but it must not be overloaded. (Diagrams for oral presentation should carry but one idea.) Remember that the diagrams, as you draw them, will be reduced in size. Study of former publications of the body to which you are subscribing will show you the size and type of diagram usually employed. You will also have had instructions from the publishers or editor as to whether they want you to complete the diagrams ready for reducing by photographic means, or whether they wish to insert numbers and words that you will indicate to them on a separate copy, in pencil. Follow these instructions carefully. Diagrams should be drawn on white paper with dense black ink if they are to reproduce well. Most societies and institutions issue pamphlets to authors giving their rules and requirements. These must be complied with if your Paper is to fit in well with the editorial policy.

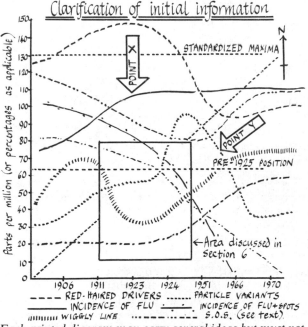

Each printed diagram may carry several ideas but must not be overloaded

The Oral Presentation

When the written Paper is out of the way, and has been sent off to the editor, you probably have several months before you are to stand up and defend what you have written. This will not be a public lecture but a fairly short period in which you will talk, and a longer period in which you will listen to the discussion of what you have said. Then, at the end, and 'off the cuff', you must stand up and answer the criticisms and the questions fired at you. You will not be popular if you say that you will reply in writing; you are expected to make a fight of it, and you have the advantage, for you probably know more about the topic than anyone else in the room. You may have the disconcerting experience at the beginning of the period of seeing a well-known authority on your topic stroll in and sit in a back row. Don't worry; he will be much more sympathetic than the brash young men near the front who wish to show the world that they know more than you!

A well-known authority on your subject may slip into the back row

We have already said that you will need to prepare a second Paper for presentation in order to prevent the audience reading your printed Paper while you are trying to talk to them. This may require some ingenuity on your part since in the printed Paper you will have arranged the reasoning behind your arguments in the best possible order. But you must never take the short cut of reading bits out of the printed version, or even of referring to its diagrams or tables. This is a recipe for losing grip of your audience: the printed Papers will again be dragged out from under the seats. You must get the attention of the audience focused on you; and the best way to do this is to produce some supporting evidence that you did not have the space to include in the Paper itself. You might also show additional photographs, radiographs, diagrams, sketches. A good way to start is to give a summary of your arguments and follow this with a short discussion on each point.

Diagrams in the Oral Presentation

Whatever method you use in this oral approach, remember that the subject is complex and you should assume that most of the audience have done no more than thumb through the pages of your Paper. Diagrams must, therefore, be simple and carry only one message. In the printed version the diagrams may carry several ideas, as we said above, because the reader has time to study them and elucidate them for himself. In the oral presentation there is no time for study. Diagrams on the screen must carry their message with a punch. That message must be self-evident to the audience because of the simplicity of your presentation. If you find that you must face the screen in order to describe and explain a diagram, you have failed. Turning your back on the audience is a very bad technique.

The use of overhead projectors allows you to face the audience as you develop a diagram on the transparent material in front of you. This is an advantage over the prepared projected slide. But make sure that you know exactly what you are to draw. Have a copy before you on the table and do not diverge from it. The lecturer who continues to poke with coloured pencils at an already finished diagram and scribbles illegible notes on it has drifted into a dream world of his own. You can prepare complete diagrams beforehand for an overhead projector but, to some extent, this lessens the advantage of this type of projector, which allows you to explain and add to diagrams bit by bit and so to hold the interest of the audience and ensure their participation. The lecturer who brings a stock of prepared transparencies and proceeds to flip them on the overhead screen in rapid succession is again using the wrong technique for effective communication. This type of presentation often consists of many complex diagrams and sketches, which no audience in a few seconds can hope to comprehend. Put yourself in the position of the audience seeing a new topic developed. What will seem childishly simple to you will require some mental adjustment and understanding by the man in the back row (even if he is the authority you saw dropping in). Keep everything simple. This means that, if you are sensible, you will not project the diagrams that appear in the paper. You will simplify them; you will use colour to make them more interesting; and you will have few of them, so that they may remain on the screen for a sufficient period for the information to sink in.

Your conduct during this period of oral presentation is a real *performance* just as if you were on a stage in a play. You know every word of your part; you are thinking of the effect on the audience all the time. You are not becoming personally interested in what you are saying, but only in its effect on your hearers. You do not *ad lib.* by putting in any interesting points that suddenly occur to you. In your practice sessions you have decided what to say and how to deal with the diagrams and pictures, and how long this will take: stick to it. The parts that suddenly occur to you can be fed into the discussion. Your oral presentation is only the opening speech for the defence!

Preparing Diagrams

The projected image on the screen should, ideally, have a vertical and lateral dimension equal to at least one-sixth of the length of the hall. This idea is not always achieved and it is well to prepare your diagrams so that they can be seen and read clearly even at greater distances than six times the screen size.

A picture occupying only a small proportion of the screen

This applies particularly to the overhead projector. Do not allow it to be placed so that it offers a picture occupying only a portion of the screen available. Move the projector so that as much as possible of the screen is used, especially if the hall is long. Remember that you are responsible for making sure that the members of the audience are in no doubt about your arguments. How often do we hear the lecturer say, after putting a complex and unreadable diagram on the screen, 'I'm afraid this is not very clear and those at the back will not be able to see it, but it shows . . . '. What a dismal failure in communication!

To have some assurance that a projected picture will at least have a chance of being readable in the circumstances available in the average hall, hold the original you have made on white paper at a distance from your eye of eight times its longest dimension. All the lettering and figures should be of such a size that they can be read easily at this distance. Since some halls will be too long, some projectors lacking in power of illumination and some screens lacking in luminance, it would be as well to lengthen this viewing distance and so make quite sure of legibility. To your eye, comparing such a diagram with the complex ones so often seen, the presentation may look ridiculously simple and large. But if the diagram is to carry its message to *all* the viewers within a few seconds, it must be instantly readable and carry a message that is crisp and clear.

'Those at the back will not be able to see this'

Think and Act

Think (A): Viewpoint

If you are asked to 'read a Paper', remember, before accepting, that this means the preparation of a report for printing, and a quite separate oral presentation that must be defended in argument. This is much harder than preparing a public lecture.

Think (B): Compliance with Controls

List the controls with which you must comply. Examples of these are: length of paper, number and size of diagrams and photographs, date of submission of written paper, projection arrangements for oral presentation and time allowed for speaking and for later replies to discussion. You must be very conscious of these controls if your performance is to be acceptable.

Act (C): Practice Sessions

The writing of the original Paper can be done in private and you can take your time in producing a good report (chapter 6). For the oral presentation, however, you are on trial before people who are knowledgeable about your subject (otherwise they would not be there). It is of the utmost importance for your later reputation that you treat the presentation as a timed and well-rehearsed performance. Go through your statements and your diagrams until you are thoroughly familiar with what you are to say and do, and then do not diverge from the programme by one iota.

Act (D): Ammunition for Defence

During the period between the preparation of the written Paper and the oral presentation, think of all the possible questions, arguments and attacks that can be fired at you. Get friends to help, and prepare the answers in written form (for jogging your memory, not for public consumption).

11
Applying for a Job

'Invent the perfect mousetrap and the world will beat a path to your door.' If any reader is in this happy position he should ignore the rest of this chapter and contact us immediately, for personal advice in exploiting his invention. (A nominal fee — say 20 per cent of realised profits — will be charged!) For the rest of you, read on.

Although *you* are fully aware of your excellent qualities and are convinced that any employer would be most fortunate to attract you to his staff, it is one of life's tragedies that in all probability *he* does not even know you exist. How to remedy that situation is a classic example of effective communication and what follows is a step-by-step guide on how to land that job of your dreams.

Applying for the Job

Let us assume that you are in your final year at college and are interested in obtaining the following advertised position. Everything about it is right — money, location, prospects etc.

> District of Northaven — Vacancy for graduate assistant engineer
> *Applications are invited for a graduate assistant post in the District Engineer's office.*
> *There is an opportunity for a young man to gain experience in design, construction of roads, bridges, sewerage, sewage-treatment works, coast protection and land reclamation.*
> *The initial appointment for a graduate assistant is withing the range of salary £X – £Z per annum but a suitable graduate could expect a salary in the region of £Y with an increment each year.*
> *Applications should be sent before June 10 1982 to:*
> *Q. Rawcliffe, B.Sc., C.Eng., F.I.C.E., District Engineer, Northaven.*

As an exercise, before going any further, close this book and write out what you would consider to be a good application.

Appalling Applications

Over the years some tutors have set this type of exercise to final-year students and, surprising as it may seem when one considers the quality and potential of the students, the following represents a typical application

> 27 Swift Terrace
> Croydon
> Sunday KT 44 LU
>
> Dear Sir
>   I am replying to your advert for
> a graduate ~~civil~~ assistant engineer.
>   I am currently completing a
> sandwich course leading to a degree in
> civil engineering during which time I have
> spent periods of industrial training
> with a motorway contractor.
>   I am, therefore, especially
> interested in the work you are offering
> in the other spheres of civil engineering as
> it will be to my advantage to have
> this experience.
>   If you require any further
> information I shall be only too
> glad to supply it.   Yours sincerely
>   J. Modest

How does your application compare? In all probability it is not much
different. Now take a cold, hard look at what you have written and ask
yourself 'Does this convey a picture that I would like others to have of me?
Would it make the employer send a telegram asking me to come at once?'
The honest answer will be No, and the reason is almost certainly that you
have not given sufficient thought to the exercise before putting pen to paper.
The employer is not concerned that the job would be to *your* advantage, and
if you have not sent *all* the necessary information — too bad; you lose,
whether you are 'only too glad' or not.

Appealing Applications

How then should you proceed? First you must establish a goal. Obviously the long-term aim is to obtain the position for which you are applying, but it is unlikely that you would obtain the position without being called for an interview in competition with others. *The immediate aim of your application is therefore to be short-listed for an interview.* Unless you are fortunate enough to have contacts within the organisation (and this is sometimes a doubtful blessing) the only means that you have available for selling yourself is the printed word in your application, and this must be exploited to the full. As previously stressed, in all exercises of communication it is essential to put yourself in the position of the person at the receiving end — here, the prospective employer. Visualise yourself in his position, and assume that the salary to finance the position is coming out of your own pocket. Now, what would you want to know from an applicant? Close the book again and write down a list of the information you would expect, and then re-open the book and compare your ideas with ours.

7 May 1982

(1) Name	John Modest
(2) Address	27 Swift Terrace, Longden, Surrey KT 99LU
(3) Date of birth	10 September 1961
(4) Marital status	Single
(5) Education	1972–1979 Longden High School
	1979–1982 Gresham University
(6) Qualifications	A-level Maths J.M.B 1978 C
	Maths J.M.B 1979 A
	Further Maths J.M.B 1979 C
	Chemistry J.M.B. 1979 D
	Physics J.M.B. 1979 B
	B.Sc. (Hons) I take my Final Honours examination in Civil Engineering in June 1982.
(7) Distinctions	(a) Head Boy, Longden High School 1978–79
	(b) School colours for cricket
	(c) Maxwell Prize for best performance in first year of undergraduate studies
(8) Relevant experience	Vacation employment
	1979 — Labourer — housing estate, Longden (6 weeks)
	1980 — Junior Engineer — Cockburn contractors, M99 motorway (10 weeks). Experience consisted mainly of helping site engineer to set out earthwork boundaries and drainage works.

	1981 — Junior Engineer — District Engineer's office, Ravenshore (10 weeks). Experience included highway design work for small housing estate and site work for 3 weeks on new sewage-disposal works during illness of senior engineer.
(9) Union and Society Activities	(a) Treasurer of the Engineering Society 1980–81 (b) Member of the following Societies: Anglican Fellowship Photographic Club Community Relations
(10) Sports and Hobbies	(a) Scoutmaster, Longden Vth Group. Attended World Jamboree in Japan in September 1978 as representative of Rover Group, Longden District. (b) Badminton (c) Bird Watching
(11) Referees	(a) Professor Bright, Dept of Civil Engineering, Gresham University (b) Rev. A. Davies, St Martin's Vicarage, Longden (c) J. Trustman, B.Sc., C.Eng., F.I.C.E. District Engineer, District Offices, Ravenshore

(Note: You must never miss a year or even part of a year in your curriculum vitae even if you were only swanning about the Greek Islands. The committee may think that you were in gaol! We have seen suspicion in the interviewing committee when dates showed a blank.)

This time, because you have made a conscious effort to think about what was required, your list and ours will probably be very similar. In filling out the information under each of these headings it is obviously advantageous to know as much as possible about the job, the organisation and the person who is likely to read and judge your application. Usually sufficient further information will be provided about the post to help you formulate a clear idea of what the job entails, but it is rarely possible to obtain information about the person who will pass judgement on your application. In the absence of such information you should assume the employer to be somewhat conservative. Without doubt he will be looking for a person of drive and initiative, with respect for authority and willing to carry responsibility. Keep that standard Identikit in mind. While it is imperative that you are completely honest in preparing your application, at the same time it must be said that it is not necessary to reveal everything about yourself. Be very selective, and tailor your application to fit the job. In other words play down those aspects that are unlikely to be considered important and highlight those that are.

Keep that standard Identikit in mind

(This is particularly important later in your career when you have more experience to draw on.) Similarly, if you are fortunate enough to have a number of referees who all think highly of you, it will probably pay to select your referees according to the position for which you are applying. However, at this stage of your career the employer will think there is something suspicious if your Head of Department or Tutor is not listed as one of your referees. Similarly, it is the usual practice to have another referee who can speak about your character in your private life. A clergyman or Justice of the Peace is an ideal person. Wherever possible ask the permission of the referee to use his name and at the same time inform him of the type of job you are applying for. A skilled referee can be selective in his comments and this can make a great deal of difference to your success or failure. Having completed your application in draft form sit back and ask yourself the following questions.

(1) Is this the best I can do?
(2) Is this the image of myself that I want to convey to my prospective employer?
(3) Have I put forward the best possible case for being called to an interview?

If not, go back and make some alterations: otherwise you must now think about the presentation.

Having set out all the information required in a sensible and orderly fashion, this is how it should be finally and formally presented. All that is necessary is a short covering letter, along the following lines, which should accompany the curriculum vitae well ahead of the closing date.

27 Swift Terrace
Longden
Surrey

7th May 1982

Dear Sir

<u>Graduate Assistant Engineer</u>

With reference to your recent advertisement for the above post, I have pleasure in enclosing my curriculum vitae.

You will see from my application that I have already had experience of working in an engineer's office and on the basis of that I have decided to make my career in the service of a local authority.

Yours faithfully

While it is permissible to write both the covering letter and the curriculum vitae in your own hand, it is regrettably true to say that the writing of many students is far from neat and is often illegible. As a general rule, therefore, the authors would recommend that the letter and curriculum vitae be typed unless, of course, an application in your own hand is specifically requested.

It is not unknown for 100 or more applications to be received for very attractive jobs, and this clearly underlines the need to present applications of the highest standard. Ideally, however, it also helps if your application is in some way physically distinctive, such that it stands out from the remaining 99 applications. Mount the curriculum vitae between cover sheets of coloured card and also bring out some very important telling point in your covering letter. For example, in the letter above, reference is made to experience already obtained in local government. Send the mounted or bound application in a large envelope; never fold it.

The technique outlined above can be used in the same way throughout the whole of your professional career. Of course, as time progresses your earlier education and qualifications such as A-level results will become less important and need not be mentioned, but greater weight will be placed on your experience and positions held. In listing your current position it is usual to mention your current salary and 'perks' (for example, car, house, etc.) and to state the period of notice you will have to serve before taking up a new appointment.

If, after taking great care over drafting your application along the lines indicated, you do not receive an invitation to join a short list then you can draw one of the following conclusions.

(1)   It's a put up job! Someone was chosen in advance — or so *you* think.

(2)   You are a suitable candidate but there are others better fitted.

(3)   You are not worthy of the position.

At least you will have the satisfaction of knowing that you have put yourself over in the best possible light. Many people have failed to get to the interview stage simply because of poor applications.

Techniques for the Interview

So you got short-listed. Well done. It paid to spend a little time and thought on the application, didn't it? Now to get the job. In replying to the letter calling you for interview be careful to maintain the same high standard of English. You cannot afford to slip up now. Clearly, you must do all in your power to attend the interview, but on rare occasions it may not be possible; you may be ill or have to attend a funeral. In such circumstances if you are still keen to get the job it is advisable to write a letter in good style and in good time (or to telephone) explaining the reasons why you cannot attend, but at the same time making it clear that you regret this since you feel you are ideally suited to the post.

Who's Who and What's What?

Before attending for interview, find out as much as you can about the organisation and the particular job. Often this can be gleaned from booklets

&CO. Ltd.

Find out as much as you can about the organisation

provided by the company, annual reports, balance sheets, published papers, etc. It is particularly important that you should be thoroughly familiar with any printed matter sent to you before you attend for interview. A committee is rightly unimpressed with a candidate who on the one hand says he wants the job and·yet, from his answers to questions, has not troubled to find out about it.

Punctuality Pleases People

Whatever your attitude to timekeeping in your personal life, remember that punctuality for your interview is of the utmost importance. It creates a very bad impression with the interviewing committee if a candidate is late in arriving — *whatever the reasons*. Because of this it is prudent to allow yourself plenty of time; you should aim to arrive at the building where the interview is to be held *at least half an hour* before the scheduled time. After locating the exact room where you have to report, then you can feel free to go to a nearby snack bar and have a coffee to steady your nerves.

Instant Impressions Important

The first minutes of any interview are of the utmost importance. During this time the committee members are forming their own private impressions of you. If these are unfavourable you will have the uphill task of changing their minds during the interview. On the other hand, if the committee is favourably impressed during the first few minutes you have won half the battle. Although you will have butterflies in your stomach, your knees will be knocking, and you will probably feel sick, brace yourself as you enter the door and put on

Choose what you think the committee would like best

your most confident (not cocky) expression. It always helps to realise at this time that every other candidate, regardless of how confident he may seem, will feel just as you do when it comes to his turn. The first impression that the committee members have of you as you enter the door is a visual one and your appearance is all-important. In choosing what clothes to wear, remember that the majority of the committee members are likely to be considerably older and rather conservative in outlook. They are, therefore, unlikely to be impressed with the latest extravagant style and you do want the job, don't you? Look in your wardrobe (such as it is) and choose according to what you think members of the committee will like best. As likely as not, this will not be what you like the most. But, although styles vary, tidiness, grooming and cleanliness do not: whatever the style of your clothes or hair, remember to be clean and tidy. Carelessness in this respect can lose you the job in the first 30 seconds. On entering the room fix your eyes on the Chairman of the committee and follow his directions carefully. If he welcomes you with a handshake, respond firmly: there is nothing worse for giving an impression of a weak character than a limp, damp hand, like a wet fish, held forward as an excuse for a handshake. Do not take a seat until asked. Usually at this stage the candidate is told the names of members of the committee. Obviously it is very impressive if you can remember the names and use them when answering questions during the interview.

A limp damp hand like a wet fish as a handshake

Informative Interview

Have with you a copy of the application you submitted and a new pencil (not chewed) to make notes. When questioned, look at the person who asked the question when replying and give clear, concise answers. Avoid giving long rambling, woolly answers, as happens all too often when a person is nervous. Don't tell all; leave something for a supplementary question. By watching the faces of the committee members it is possible to detect their reactions and you can soon judge if you are talking too much. By keeping your finger on the pulse of the meeting it is even possible to guide some of the questions in the direction you want. For example, if you have some particularly strong points that you wish to mention and these are not being asked for in the questions, then by skilful answers to the current question it is often possible to bring the conversation round to the points you want to make.

When asked a question during the interview never say you are not quite sure what the questioner means and would he kindly explain. This puts the questioner in a bad light *vis-à-vis* his colleagues on the board. Making him lose face in this way is likely to lose you his vote. He is not there to explain to you. Answer something to the question and he may follow up with a supplementary from which you can develop an argument in the right direction.

It is common practice at the end of the interview for the Chairman to ask the candidate if he has any questions he would like to ask the committee. This is an opportunity to take command of the situation. If you ask no questions it looks as though you have no ideas and if you ask too many and go rambling on it is clear that you are lacking in judgement since, although the Chairman asked for questions, he really didn't expect many. The right course of action is to have a few questions ready before you enter the room and choose the most suitable and appropriate. If by any chance all the questions that you prepared have been dealt with, say something like: 'I found the interview to be most helpful since you cleared up a large number of points I had but could you just please clarify . . . ' Incidentally when starting out on your career you should avoid questions on holidays and pension schemes! It gives the impression that you are tired out before you start.

Definite and Delayed Decisions

Sometimes a committee will arrive at a decision the same day, and will invite the successful candidate back into the room to inform him of its decision; at this stage they may also discuss such things as salary and starting date, where these have not been dealt with earlier. Although this is a thrilling moment, it can also be a tricky one to handle if for any reason you are not prepared to accept the appointment immediately. On this point we are of the opinion that, if the the offer is not substantially different from what you could reasonably expect from the advertisement and the further particulars sent to you, you should be prepared to make a decision there and then. Anyone worth his salt will have thought about all the implications before coming for interview. Don't say, at this late stage, that you must discuss it with your wife, husband, uncle or mother. *That should have been done before you applied.* If during the course of the interview it becomes apparent that the position itself or the conditions of appointment are substantially different, however, you are justified in asking for a few days in which to make a decision. You should apologise for having to delay the decision, but at the same time politely give your reasons and also an undertaking to let them have a definite decision within seven days or so. Keep your promise. Finally, whatever happens in the final interview, you should aim to leave the committee members with the feeling that they have indeed appointed the right person.

Congratulations and Condolences

So you got the job of your dreams — congratulations. However, if by any remote chance you didn't, no morbid recriminations please. One of the qualities of a successful professional person is the ability to learn from failures, and this situation is no exception. Constructively go over the interview and, if you made errors, determine not to repeat them next time. It could be, of course, that the successful candidate had already read this book!

Think and Act

Think (A): Viewpoint

Despite the title of this chapter, your application is not for a job but for an *interview!*

Think (B): Appealing Application Not Appalling

So far as the interviewing panel is concerned, your curriculum vitae is *you*. No detail about you or your circumstances can be omitted. This is the one occasion when you may boast of your achievements without incurring censure. Make the most of it.

Act (C): Outstanding Application

Write down ten ways in which your application can be made to stand out and be noticed at a glance when submerged in a pile of others. The panel may wish to look at your curriculum vitae for a second assessment. 'The application was in a blue cover with red spots, if I remember correctly,' says the Chairman and fishes it out easily. What about the other nine ways?

Act (D): Questions to Ask

Write down three questions that, at the end of the interview, you may wish to put to the Chairman. You must choose subjects that will show your interest in the job, and phrase each question so that it raises you in the estimation of the panel. Take time over framing these questions; do not leave it to the moment when the Chairman asks if you would like to make any comments. We were on a panel once when a candidate, who up to that moment had seemed well suited to the university post he sought, asked the suicidal question: 'What are the holidays?' The Chairman glared and growled: 'Young man, there are *no* holidays.' And there was no appointment either!

12
Pushing Out

The techniques of speaking and writing, which occupy the earlier chapters, are related to tasks that you will encounter chiefly during your education and training. But communication is a complex craft and there are many minor techniques that you will find it advisable to master. For example, we have said nothing about correspondence and dictation, especially the dictation into a tape recorder for typing by an audio typist. As a first-stage communication from person to person this demands a technique of a higher order than is at first apparent if you are looking for a first-class result. Also, we have not had space to write about the craft of correcting printers' proofs. You will have to do this if you have any concern with pamphlets, advertisements, programmes, handbills, brochures or books. Printers have their own symbols for communicating with exactitude what corrections are to be made to the printed text. They are shown in British Standard 5261:Part 1:1975 and Part 2:1977. Unless you use this language, your communication with the printer will be faulty; your own private symbols will only mislead. Look for and study minor techniques; they will stand you in good stead.

But this chapter is concerned chiefly with your progress in communication in later years, when you have taken up a post in industry or the professions. We shall call you by that popular all-embracing word *executive*, which includes the professional, the businessman and the professors and teachers whom we had occasion to mention in earlier chapters. You cannot become an effective executive overnight; it takes much practice. Throughout the book we have recommended that you practise the techniques of communication regularly while still at college. Suppose, then, that you are several steps ahead of your contemporaries when you start communicating in business or the professions. What further crafts must you acquire; what must you observe and note?

Personality — an Executive Asset

As a junior executive, your communication will still lie chiefly in the fields of writing and speech. But, more importantly, you will be communicating *yourself* much more positively than you had to do at college. Now your actions are not confined to the study, the writing desk or the silent library. You will be in frequent personal communication with other people. The periods of these communications may be short, but colleagues and superiors will be observing and assessing you. Ask yourself the questions: 'Do I convey a good impression? Do I convey any impression at all?' Students at College may be divided into two main categories — *memorable* and *non-memorable*. The first were those who made an impression by having a strong personality, showing brilliance, or being a source of trouble. The non-memorable passed on like wraiths, leaving no impression behind. Unless you transmit and communicate to others a personality that is clearly and unmistakeably *you*, your progress will not be fast.

To start on the highest grade of communication — transmitting *yourself* — you must first become self-conscious. This word has come to mean 'bashful, shy and awkward' because inexperienced people, realising they are being observed and assessed, are suddenly conscious of their personality and feel it is lacking. They become disturbed. In this chapter the word is meant to convey the impression that *you must always be aware of your personality* and of how you look to other people — not only when you are giving a lecture, presenting a report or introducing visitors to your superior, but at all times. To be bashful and embarrassed is a kind of pride or vanity, for you put yourself in a more prominent position than you really occupy in the mind of the observer. Observe yourself continuously; take note of what you find; reject and alter what is not acceptable as a 'good personality'. Keep the word 'self-conscious' in your mind. Don't accept the oft-repeated statement that you cannot alter your personality: this is nonsense. A substantial part of your personality came from influences that controlled your development after infancy. It is not easy to re-build yourself, but it is possible. The younger you start, the easier it is.

Aspects of Personality

The five aspects of personality that we have selected below are, in our opinion, the most important for your success. From these, others appear. You gain more confidence in your own abilities; you build up enthusiasm and interest in your work and you conquer the executive's enemy of worry and stress.

The mnemonic is TRIAD, which reminds you of *Temperament, Responsibility, Integrity, Appearance* and *Delegation*.

T: Temperament and Control

As an executive, you wish to communicate to others an acceptable personality; start then by developing a consistent temperament. Nothing should 'put you out', upset you or make you lose your temper, and you should display any desirable qualities you have with consistency in all circumstances. In times of crisis and stress, you should work coolly and logically without being swayed by temperamental or emotional disturbance. We knew a young professional photographer whose garage caught fire so that his car was completely destroyed. By the time he was aroused from sleep the fire had gained control. Most people would have been too upset to think clearly and logically. But, he reached for his camera, approached the inferno and took pictures that he sold to the press for a welcome sum. This is the kind of control of temperament required by an executive or professional person.

No mechanism in modern life is acceptable if it goes out of control. The television set that shows a distorted picture, the washing machine that does not keep to its programme and the heating boiler that does not stay alight are brought back into control as fast as possible. Yet it is often accepted as normal that *you* should be allowed to go out of control without comment or correction. If you are known to bang the table and shout, or if your staff anxiously examine your face to see whether you are in Mood 3 or Mood 16, then you must become more self-conscious and examine your temperament. Perhaps you pride yourself on being 'blunt', saying exactly what you think, regardless of the effect your statements may have on others. You say, with a shrug of the shoulders, 'Of course, I fly off the handle now and then, but what of it? It's better than bottling up grudges.' This attitude shows crude insensitivity to the feelings of others; it is chimerical to imagine that there is only a choice between flying off the handle and bottling up grudges. Both are unacceptable in a controlled and balanced executive. Be in charge of yourself so that no situation can overpower your control. If your temperament is unbalanced and likely to go out of control this flaw in your personality will not go unnoticed.

R: Responsibility

An executive accepts responsibility readily. Responsibility brings with it accountability to some superior; it means that you must carry the blame if things go wrong, even if the direct mistake is made by one of your juniors and you, personally, were not involved. One of your important tasks is to learn to select staff who also feel a sense of responsibility — that the job must be done well regardless of personal inconvenience. Nothing, except perhaps integrity, is more valued in an executive than the ability to accept responsibility and inspire his staff to do the same. The reporting and feedback that we mentioned in earlier chapters comes into play here, for it is of prime importance in communication that the senior person who assigned you the task is informed of its progress. Similar feedback must come to you from your juniors if responsibility is not only carried but seen to be carried well.

I: Integrity

Of all the qualities required by an executive, integrity is, without doubt, of supreme importance. As a successful executive you must be completely trustworthy and honest. These qualities can be developed deliberately by attention to detail. To maintain integrity as part of your proved personality means that you will, on occasion, be subjected to self-imposed inconvenience in the carrying out of a promise, or in the keeping of an appointment. Is your word to be accepted as a bond? Can you be relied on in small things as well as in the larger aspects of executive life? When you make an appointment are you always punctual, or do you find yourself saying, 'Awfully sorry I'm late'? If you have been given a deadline for the presentation of a report do you put everything else aside, even at great inconvenience, to keep within the time-table allowed? Not many people can be trusted to act promptly, punctually and consistently, in accordance with promises or duties. A trustworthy executive goes far; an executive without integrity fails.

A: Appearance

One of the interesting facets of the study of costume is how the sporting and casual wear of one generation becomes the formal wear some decades or centuries later. In the late eighteenth century, gentlemen's long coats, which were buttoned down the front, started to be cut away so as to allow for comfort on horseback and the unrestrained handling of the reins. The gradual change in this costume to the 'white tie and tails' of the twentieth century — the dress for very formal occasions — passed smoothly through the decades, and the absurdities of the transfer went unnoticed. Not only is the dress of formal evening cut away in front to allow the use of reins, but the tails of the coat are adapted to the posterior of the gallant mount! Today the changes from casual to formal attire are more rapid than in the past and this acceleration poses problems for you in your advance towards higher executive status. Only 40 years ago, denims (jeans) were worn by American cowboys when cleaning out the stables. Now, as we write, the costume is seen everywhere and accepted for evening occasions and television interviews. The casual has become formal once again, but at a rate disturbing to many whose personal time-scale has not accelerated to the same extent. Some people, of course, are not expected to move as fast as youth in sartorial revolution. The Prime Minister would not attend a Bankers' dinner in denims today, but it may be no surprise if he does so in a decade or two.

It took a century for the fashion of short hair for men of the sixteenth century to change to the political distinction between short hair for Puritans and long hair for Royalists. Then, the progression through the perukes of Pepys' time and the enormous wigs of the eighteenth century to the hirsute appearances of our Victorian ancestors, and back again to the short hair of the early twentieth century, took another 300 years. Today, 300 years after the Civil War, long and short hair for men again take on a pseudo-political connotation. First used as a signal of 'opting out' of society, long hair later became merely an indication of protest and non-comformity. But such is the pressure to comform with non-comformity, and so rapid has the spread of the fashion been, that the non-conformity signal is being flown by those who have no intention of being rebels.

Clothes and hair act as signals (as women have realised for centuries) which illustrate your inner convictions and your way of looking at life. A ship flies signal flags to communicate its status and activity. You fly similar signals by your costume. A stout businessman in shorts, sandals and a bright floppy shirt is signalling, 'I am on holiday! I don't have to work today'. To any executive who has worked in industry for only a short time all this is self-evident; he knows the signals that he must fly. To you, however, the importance of the signals of dress, and to a lesser extent, of hair styles, is worthy of serious thought. From the safe haven of college, where any sartorial or hirsute extravagance is accepted as merely signalling to a different world that you are still a callow student, you must now adapt your signals to the environment in which you will be sailing.

If you wear casual clothes when presenting yourself for interview, you are just the same person as you would be if dressed in the most formal attire, but your signal is wrong. You will have the same treatment as a vessel flying the quarantine flag. You are saying, in effect, 'I am so capable and suited to the post that my mind does not descend to such trival matters as dress. My brilliance is unmistakable and can be appreciated whatever costume I wear.' This is a dangerous signal and one not likely to be appreciated by an interviewing panel. Of course, it is illogical that they should show sympathy to your application if you wear one costume, but reject it if you wear another: you are the same person. But in rejecting convention (convention is one way of achieving politeness) you would be illustrating an insensitivity to human reactions. This insensitivity would, if carried forward into your job, have possibly dangerous repercussions in the organisation, and the interviewers cannot take the risk. Think more about the signals you fly as you communicate with others through appearance.

D: Delegation

This word is much used in management studies. It is a corollary of responsibility and indicates not only an action on your part, but also a state of mind. One of the most dangerous catch phrases on which to base your attitudes to responsibility is: 'If you want a thing done well, do it yourself.' Acceptance of this specious philosophy as truth has been the cause of many ulcers; thrombosis thrives on the pressure under which you exist (not live) if you believe this nonsense. If you are submerged in detailed work and have not a minute to call your own, it is probably your own fault. If you visit one of the top industrialists in his office you will probably find a cleared desk and no sign of pressure or stress. In the offices under his charge a similar unpressurised progress obtains. This condition is reached by skilled delegation.

Delegation is the relinquishing of direct personal action in the detailed work of your department or organisation. Delegation must be planned minutely at first, if it is to be successful, but once the plan has been made and phases of the work delegated, the detail goes to others. Do not interfere, if you are the one who has passed on the distributed tasks. There is nothing more depressing or more likely to weaken the support of your staff than for a young person to be given some task of responsibility, only to find that the boss has started on the job himself, or that he continually checks and inspects detail. Ask for regular reports if they are necessary, but otherwise keep clear if delegation by you is to be successful. You will have loyal and effective support if you show confidence in your juniors.

Nothing more depressing than to find that the boss continually checks

It is unfortunately true that you may be let down. But then it is not the principle of delegation that is at fault, rather your ability in assessing personality and temperament: you have picked the wrong person. You will gradually learn how to assess character; it is a very difficult craft, but one that must be mastered if delegation — an aspect of communication — is to be successful.

Remember, you can control directly only a few people. They, in their turn, have their pattern of delegation. If you have four or five people who report directly to you, and for whose work you are accountable, this is as much as you should consider to be manageable. Think carefully round these ideas and draw a pattern diagram showing your responsibilities and their delegation among your juniors (see chapter 4).

Making Decisions

We make decisions continuously; it is a daily task for all of us, from deciding what's to be cooked for dinner to clinching a merger of companies. The making of effective decisions or the accurate solving of problems — merely another way of stating the same issue — depends on logical and controlled thought, and is certainly not easy. Making decisions and acting on them represents one of the highest forms of communication, and requires all the concentration and attention that you can apply.

An eminent industrialist, drawing on his wide experience, used to say that no decision can be made nor should be attempted until all the facts are assembled. But, he said, when you have all the facts, a decision can be made in one minute. This did not mean that only one minute's thought should be applied to the problem, but only that the last items of data finally allowed a proper choice to be made between possible alternatives, which had already been put on a short list of solutions. The compilation of such a short list from which the final decisions can be selected is accomplished by techniques long accepted and studied. As a crash course in decision-making and problem-solving, we give you a few ideas well known to anyone who has tackled this aspect of the executive's responsibility. To make your task easier we have devised still another mnemonic. (Are you tired of them yet?) It is COOT: *Circulate, Open mind, Orientation, Talk with colleagues*.

Why do we so often find difficulty in making a sound decision when faced by some problem? There are several main reasons: we fail to use every item of information that we have collected; we do not collect all the information and data that we should; we do not examine the data carefully enough; and we often get our mind stuck in a groove so that, in considering a problem, we find difficulty in moving our attention from the first approach that came into our minds. In short, we do not look at a sufficient number of alternatives.

C: Circulate and Re-arrange

Be sure that you have all the facts and data relating to the problems on which you must make a decision. Do not at this stage make any steps towards a solution or you may be trapped mentally in the strait-jacket of one dominant idea. No idea must be dominant at this stage. Write down each of the facts on which you must eventually base your decision, and circulate them. They can each be written on a separate card and these cards moved around on a table. The aim is to ensure that you know the limits within which you are to work in making a decision and that you are thoroughly familiar with all the facts available to help you.

Look at the way in which the problem has been presented to you. The order in which basic facts, probabilities, questions and relationships between data are presented is quite fortuitous, in order of size or in some other way. If you allow the order of presentation to influence your thinking at this stage you may well find that you take much longer to reach the solution. When, eventually, the solution does appear you will say, 'Why didn't I think of that before?' The answer is that you allowed your judgement to be directed and influenced by the arrangement of the presentation as it reached you. You must be free of all trammels as you enter the decision-making stage. To accomplish this, make sure that you re-arrange and circulate items of data until they have lost any form of pre-arranged order. Your mind is then sufficiently free to start the next stage.

O: Open mind

Having assessed, understood and circulated the data on which you must build, your next step is to draw a pattern diagram (chapter 4). Several diagrams of this kind may be possible; if so, develop them all to some extent before making a choice of one or the other. One route to a solution may then become apparent, but remember that it may not be the only route. The pressure to find a solution or to come to a decision — any decision — will begin to be so strong that you can become biased, against your will, to your first solution. This bias should be avoided; keep an open mind.

Now reject completely, but temporarily, the pattern diagram that seems most nearly to be complete, and go on to the others in an attempt to build up several possible solutions. These answers to the problem are in competition to be selected for a short list; they must be left free to make their own case as your thinking progresses.

O: Orientation

Even with the open plan of progress detailed above, you may often come to a dead end. You can see no further towards a decision nor make a choice between alternatives. This is not the result of neglecting facts or of not keeping an open mind, but rather of the orientation of your thinking. If you have been writing notes to guide your progress, change to figures or sketches. If you have tried a pattern diagram try a numerical solution. Looking at a problem from a different orientation often results in a gleam of light in a dark area.

In chapter 7 we emphasised the importance of reading the whole examination paper before attempting to answer it, so that the sub-conscious mind could work on the facts presented and bring to the conscious level the possible methods of attack for the various questions. In the same way, if a decision seems to hang fire, present your facts to the sub-conscious and give up conscious work on the problem. Leave any decision in abeyance for some time. On coming back to the task later, you are likely to find that you have sub-consciously achieved a fresh orientation and a new outlook: the solution is nearer.

Discussion with others can overcome a block in your thinking

T: Talk with colleagues

In chapter 2 we pointed out that, in college work, there is too little use of oral discussion. We recommended that you should get together with friends for group sessions of oral discussion on specific topics of study. In making decisions or solving the problems facing an executive, the same principle applies. Discussion with others is a powerful means of overcoming a block in your own thinking. Make up a rough agenda for such discussion sessions so that the subject can be ventilated. Problems should always be discussed with the people most closely concerned and, when you cannot find a solution yourself, clarification by discussion is even more important.

A Test for You

Have a go at this one!

> *The vicar problem*: A vicar says to his curate, 'I have three parishioners, the product of their ages being 2450 and the sum twice your own age. How old are the parishioners?' The curate thinks a while and then points out that he hasn't sufficient information to solve the problem. At this, the vicar gives him a further clue, and assures him that he now has enough information to give the correct answer. The further clue is that the vicar is older than any of the three parishioners. 'Ah,' says the curate, 'now I can give you the parishioners' ages'. *Your problem* is to find the age of the vicar.

This is a superb little problem which can be solved in three or four minutes by a good logical mind. See how long it takes you. There is no need for us to give you the solution. If you get the correct answer you will know. If, on the other hand, you are tempted to ask 'Is it . . .?' you haven't solved the problem. If you are really stuck look on p. 170 — but don't cheat! Remember integrity?

Keeping Up with the Joneses

This well-known phrase has overtones which suggest that there are advantages in doing what the Joneses do. This is an interesting concept in the context of this chapter, which deals with communication through personality and by action. If the behaviour of the Joneses is so important as to merit a catch phrase, you would do well to enquire what makes their communication so effective and attractive. Have they succeeded in finding some valuable communicative technique not touched on in this book?

The example displayed by the Joneses may sometimes be trivial — concerning, perhaps, new forms of house decoration or personal costume. Such, however, is the power of the Jones's example that, instead of being rejected for being different, they quietly become leaders. You will find that, in a little time, those who don't conform to the lead of the Joneses are looked upon as non-conformist — unless they are also Joneses themselves.

What kind of people do you think they are? Is it worth following their lead? How do they manage to exert such influence? Careful research by Cassie and Constantine has uncovered some of the Jones's principles and six of the more important are given below. If *you* continue the research, we are sure you will find other characteristics of the Joneses which account for their phenomenal influence on society today.

The Joneses and the Questioning Mind

Our research has shown that the Joneses are never in an apathetic frame of mind. They are always questioning: 'What would happen if . . . ?'; 'Suppose we did . . . ?'; 'How are we to get . . . ?' Cross-questioning is constant, and from this maelstrom of queries come new ideas which make the non-Jones faction furious and amazed. 'Why didn't we think of that? Now we'll have to follow if we want to maintain our exports!'

The Joneses ask questions and build the answers.

The Joneses and the Logical Outlook

Solving problems comes naturally to the Joneses. They muster the facts and data, assess the questions being asked, proceed to a logical study, find the action required and make a decision. They always have the evidence to support it. They have the *second report* described in chapter 6.

The Joneses make firm decisions.

The Joneses and Worry

No Jones ever says, in a self-satisfied tone and with a merry shrug, 'Well, I've always been a worrier; can't help it.' Worry militates against clear decisions and the Joneses have long realised that their influence would be very weak if they allowed the unrewarding turning over and over in the mind of multitudinous detail to cloud their clear decisions.

The Joneses abandoned worry long ago.

The Joneses and Change

The Joneses never say, 'But it's always been done that way.' Nor do they say, 'I've carried out this job like this for 20 years: I know what I'm doing.' If, as a result of their questioning attitude, they see that some improvement might be made, they are not inhibited in making a change. The state of things as they are is never held in awe by the Joneses merely because it has lasted for decades.

The Joneses have no fear of necessary innovation.

The Joneses and Communication

The Joneses use every means of communication, but they transmit their ideas chiefly by personality and example. They are first-class communicators; their ideas spread with speed, often against the flow of accepted opinion. Their imitators follow but never catch up. While others are making a Jones-change, the Joneses are already working on another problem.

The Joneses are always ahead.

The Joneses are always ahead

The Joneses and Public Opinion

If the Joneses followed public opinion blindly, they would not be able to exert their undoubted influence. 'What will the neighbours think?' is not one of the questions asked by the Joneses. They have their own well-founded and carefully considered opinions. It is surprising how many others find the actions of the Joneses right for them too, but at a later date. To the criticisms directed by public opinion, the Joneses repeat the motto carved in an archway of Marischal College, in the ancient University of Aberdeen.

This motto divides its message into three, which we recommended as a good technique in chapter 9. Each panel has an admonitory hand pointing to the old lettering, with thumb and forefinger making a V-sign of Victory. It must have been devised by one of the Jones family!

Nothing could be more confident or more scornful.

No need exists in this chapter for **Think and Act**. We have said our last word. We wish you well.

Index

Solution to the Vicar Problem

The curate has the following information

$$P_1 \times P_2 \times P_3 = 2450$$

$$P_1 + P_2 + P_3 = 2 \times \text{curate's ages}$$

Curate knows his own age

Since he cannot decide on the ages of the parishioners, it follows that he is faced with a solution which is not unique. A quick analysis of the prime factors of 2450 ($7 \times 7 \times 5 \times 5 \times 2 \times 1 \times 1$) shows that the only solutions are

$$5 + 10 + 49 = 64 \qquad 5 \times 10 \times 49 = 2450$$

$$7 + 7 + 50 = 64 \qquad 7 \times 7 \times 50 = 2450$$

Given that the vicar is older than any of the parishioners and having the assurance that the curate now has sufficient information to solve the problem, he knows that the parishioners' ages are 5, 10 and 49 and therefore the vicar is 50. If he were older than 50 the curate would not have been able to decide between the solutions 5, 10 and 49, and 7, 7 and 50. If on the other hand he were younger than 50 there would be no solution at all.